Please renew or return items by the date
shown on your receipt

www.hertsdirect.org/libraries

Renewals and
enquiries: 0300 123 4049

Textphone for hearing   0300 123 4041
or speech impaired

WHO GOES HOME?

WHO GOES HOME?

A Parliamentary Miscellany

ROBERT ROGERS

The Robson Press

First published in Great Britain in 2012 by
The Robson Press (an imprint of Biteback Publishing Ltd)
Westminster Tower
3 Albert Embankment
London SE1 7SP
Copyright © Robert Rogers 2012

ISBN 978-1-84954-396-5

10 9 8 7 6 5 4 3 2 1

A CIP catalogue record for this book is available from the British Library.

Set in Chronicle

Printed and bound in Great Britain by
CPI Group (UK) Ltd, Croydon CRO 4YY

To Jane, Catherine and Eleanor, as always

CONTENTS

ACKNOWLEDGEMENTS

Many of the illustrations in this book come from the Parliamentary Works of Art Collection. The Works of Art Collection documents the history of Parliament, its people, buildings and activities through history to the present day. For further information, and to search the Collection, go to www.parliament.uk/art

Most of the documents pictured in this book come from the Parliamentary Archives, which holds the historic records of the House of Commons and House of Lords from 1497 to the present day, and makes them available to the public. For further information, and to search the Archives catalogue, go to www.parliament.uk/archives

FOREWORD

Who Goes Home? – usually abbreviated to a long, drawn-out *Ho-o-o-o-o-me* – is shouted by the doorkeepers of the House of Commons at the end of each day's sitting. In less law-abiding days it was a rallying cry for homeward-bound Members to band together for mutual protection against highwaymen and footpads. (In the twenty-first century, for 'footpads' perhaps read 'journalists'…)

Everyone who works in, or visits, the Palace of Westminster is constantly reminded of how the old lives with the new. I think we are pretty comfortable with this; history should be our inspiration, not our jailer. This parliamentary miscellany reflects the long history of Parliament and of the Palace. Although much changes, much remains the same. Parliamentary alliances and feuds of 300 years ago have a familiar ring to them; sacking ministers in the Victorian era has a modern resonance; spin is nothing new; and virtue and vice, wit and insult, success and failure, are constants.

I acknowledged in the Foreword to this book's predecessor, *Order! Order!*, the debt I owe to other anthologists: those who have tracked and cornered the prey to allow others to catch up, and that is a debt I am still happy to acknowledge. But, now as then, the majority of the material in this book comes from a box which, over four decades at Westminster, I have been filling with the curious and surprising, the witty, the scorching and the plain unhinged.

In each chapter I embark upon a theme but quickly lose it. That seems reasonable in a miscellany. There is more about the Commons than the Lords, but I have spent forty years at the Commons end of the Palace.

As with *Order! Order!* I owe a great debt to Melanie Unwin, Deputy Curator of Works of Art, and to Mari Takayanagi, Archivist at the Parliamentary Archives, for their expertise and enthusiasm in identifying suitable illustrations; and I am grateful for permission to reproduce those of the illustrations which are Parliamentary copyright. The guidance of Richard Hilliard, an old friend and fascinated (and sometimes disbelieving) observer of Parliament has been welcome as always; and I am once again very grateful to Richard Cracknell, Head of Social Statistics in the House of Commons Library, for his help in turning historical sums of money into modern equivalents.

I am also very grateful to Ian Denyer, Peter Hennessy, Robin James, Liam Laurence Smyth, Caroline Nicholls,

John Pullinger, Peter Riddell and Andrew Tremlett for their contributions. I owe particular thanks to Jeremy Robson, my publisher, especially for his expert enthusiasm, to Lewis Carpenter, for his hard work, and to Charlotte Howard, my agent, for her splendid support.

Order! Order! was published in 2009, an unhappy year for Parliament, and a sad time for those of us who have spent our working lives explaining the institution and trying to make it more effective. But the 2010 General Election was a sea change. It brought in 227 new Members of Parliament who, with their returning colleagues, were determined to make it a different place. Parliament is more active, self-confident and relevant than I have ever seen it; and this is the best possible basis for engagement with its real owners, the people of the United Kingdom.

Robert Rogers
Westminster
September 2012

THE PALACE ON THORNEY ISLAND

A terrible place.

Description, in a charter of King Offa, of Thorney Island
(the Island of Thorns) where the Palace of Westminster
and Westminster Abbey now stand.

❧

The magnificent Westminster Hall, the most ancient part
of the Palace of Westminster, was built to its present size
– 240 ft by 69 ft (73m by 21m) by William Rufus between
1097 and 1099. Between 1394 and 1401 the Norman walls
were refaced, heightened by 2 ft and buttressed by Henry
Yevele so that they could take the weight of the huge oak
roof designed by Hugh Herland.

In 2012–15 a major and long overdue programme
of repair and conservation is tackling the stonework,
masonry and roof, and for the first time lighting the highest parts of the Hall properly.

Unsurprisingly for such an ancient building in such a place, the Hall has been repaired and tinkered with in most centuries since the eleventh. In 2011 the most recent survey found that no fewer than nine types of stone had been used:

- Reigate (mediaeval, and in 1820)
- Caen (mediaeval)
- A magnesian limestone, possibly Marre (mediaeval)
- Huddleston (1834)
- Painswick (1850)
- Hopton Wood (1850)
- Ketton (1888 and 1949)
- Portland (1888)
- Mansfield White/Cadeby (date unknown).

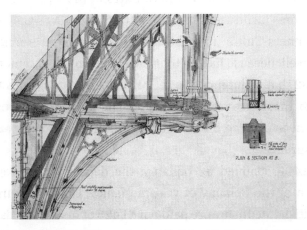

A roof truss in Westminster Hall, by Sir Frank Baines, the architect who worked on Westminster Hall 1914–23

The foundations of the eleventh-century Hall were of Kentish ragstone set in lime mortar, ballast and lime concrete, just over 12 ft deep in the gravel of Thorney Island.

INSURANCE CLAIMS

The fire of 16 October 1834 burned down much of the Palace of Westminster, and the heritage of centuries was lost. Some of the inhabitants of the Palace lost personal possessions, too; three years later they were still seeking compensation from an ungenerous government, on the grounds that the negligence of government servants (the workmen who had enthusiastically piled the tally sticks into the furnace that heated the House of Lords) had caused their loss.

£9,000: Charles Manners-Sutton, the Speaker, for his fine furniture (about £830,000 in today's money). Manners-Sutton must have been annoyed with himself as well, because having told the House in the summer of 1832 that he intended to retire, he let his policy with the Sun Insurance Company lapse. The new Whig government persuaded him to stay on, but he didn't renew the insurance.

£400: claimed by Bellamy, the deputy housekeeper (son of the Bellamy of veal pie fame). He was insured; British Life Insurance paid out £1,425 of his £1,500 claim but Bellamy held the government responsible for another £400, or about £37,000 in today's money.

£1.12s.6d. (£1.62 ½ pence, or about £150 today): claimed by William Bevan, a messenger, for a dress hat at 10s.6d, a pair of court shoes at 10s.0d, and a pair of buckles at 12s.0d.

The Destruction by Fire of the Houses of Parliament, 16 October 1834, by William Gauci

THE WOOLSACK...

...is the rectangular red bench in the House of Lords, like a misshapen sofa, on which the Lord Speaker (and for centuries before, the Lord Chancellor) sits. There has probably been a Woolsack since the fourteenth century, and it is thought to have indicated the importance of the wool trade to England. Over the years, its stuffing changed to horsehair, but in 1938 it was restuffed with wool from England, Scotland, Wales, Northern Ireland and the Commonwealth.

THE TILT ON THE ELIZABETH TOWER

In July 2012 the Clock Tower was formally renamed the Elizabeth Tower to mark the Queen's Diamond Jubilee, complementing the Victoria Tower at the south end of the Palace. The Elizabeth Tower houses the Great Clock and its hour bell Big Ben; it leans to the north-west 0.26 degrees out of the vertical or 1 ft 5in. (435mm) from the vertical at the top of the Tower (315 ft or 96m). The tilt has increased very slightly in recent years to 0.9mm a year rather than 0.65mm a year. But at present rates it would take about 4,000 years to catch up with the Leaning Tower of Pisa, which leans 4 degrees.

Why are we squeezed into so small a space that it is absolutely impossible that there should be calm and regular discussion... Why do we live in this hubbub?... Why are 658 of us crammed into a space which allows to each of us no more than a foot and a half square?

William Cobbett in 1833, the year before much of the Palace burned down

OSCAR NEMON

The statue of Churchill in the Members' Lobby of the House of Commons, unveiled on 1 December 1969, was the work of the great sculptor Oscar Nemon (1906–85). It was intended to portray Churchill striding through the rubble of war-torn London. Churchill's widow complained that the rubble at the foot of the statue didn't look realistic. As the statue was already cast in bronze, Nemon added some fibreglass rubble to please Lady Churchill.

Soon after the statue was unveiled, a practice grew up (after only a few years it became a hallowed tradition) of Conservative MPs touching Churchill's foot before key speeches or great occasions – and thousands of visitors to Westminster followed suit. The bronze finish soon wore off to reveal a golden shoe. Nemon used to come in from time to time to paint the shoe brown again.

Oscar Nemon used to use other people as models for his statues when the famous subjects had little time for long sittings. The policeman on duty outside St James's Palace, near Nemon's studio, posed for Churchill's legs. And a stand-in for the statue of Lord Portal of Hungerford outside the Ministry of Defence was Nemon's son-in-law, Sir George Young, later Leader of the House of Commons.

In the 1930s the Palace of Westminster burned 80 tons of coal a week.

THE GREAT STINK
In July 1855 Michael Faraday took a steamboat along the Thames. He had recently returned from the coun-tryside and was all the more appalled and outraged by the condition of the river. The great scientist wrote to *The Times*:

The whole of the river was an opaque brown fluid. Surely

the river which flows for so many miles through London ought not to be allowed to become a fermenting sewer?

Disraeli described the river as '*a Stygian pool, reeking with ineffable and unbearable horrors*'.

The state of the river was not just an affront to the senses. In 1854, 616 people died of cholera after drinking water from a pump on Broad Street that had been contaminated by a cesspit. That outbreak was the one that famously allowed John Snow to establish for the first time that cholera is a water-borne disease, and it was by no means the worst. An outbreak in 1848–49 had killed at least 14,000 people.

The 'fermenting sewer' was all too well known in one building on its banks. Charles Barry's new Palace of Westminster stank as well. Chloride of lime was used to soak curtains and sheets hung in front of the windows. The 'noxious stench' was so bad that there were thoughts of Parliament moving to Oxford or St Albans.

STATE OF THE THAMES – QUESTION

MR BRADY said, he wished to put a question to the noble Lord the Chief Commissioner of Works with regard to the state of the Thames. It was a notorious fact that hon. Gentlemen sitting in the Committee Rooms and the Library were utterly unable to remain there in consequence of the stench which arose from the river; and he wished to know if the noble Lord had taken any measures for mitigating the effluvium and discontinuing the nuisance.

Lord JOHN MANNERS said, he was very sorry to tell the hon. Gentleman that the River Thames was not in his jurisdiction, and therefore not under his control.

Hansard, 11 June 1858

STATE OF THE THAMES – QUESTION

Mr MANGLES: I wish to ask the noble Lord the Chief Commissioner of Works whether he intends to take any steps with regard to the present state of the River Thames? [Laughter and cheers.] *My question, I perceive, excites the laughter of some hon. Gentlemen, but I can assure them that if they lived in the vicinity of the Thames they would not think my question one of little importance. By a perverse ingenuity, one of the noblest of rivers has been changed into a cesspool, and I wish to ask whether Her Majesty's Government intend to take any steps to remedy the evil?*

Hansard, 15 June 1858

The government did intend to take steps. In time-honoured fashion, the steps consisted of ... a select committee to recommend solutions! But this select committee did find an answer: making the Metropolitan Board of Works responsible for the purification of the Thames; in 1859 the chief engineer of the Board, Joseph Bazalgette, proposed and then began work on a huge underground sewage system for London. The 82 miles of sewers, including the vast Victoria, Albert and Chelsea Embankments, caught human waste before it could reach the Thames and then pumped it out to sea. Bazalgette estimated the maximum flow the sewers would have to carry, and then doubled it. After the system was completed in 1875, the threat of cholera never threatened again. Bazalgette received a well-merited knighthood.

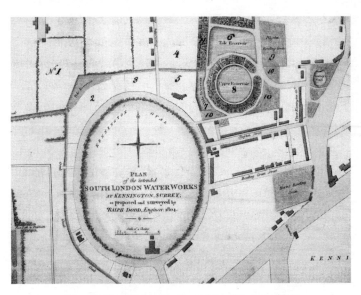

Plan of the Waterworks at Kennington, 1804

FLAGS

Since January 2010 the flag on the Victoria Tower at the south end of the Palace of Westminster flies every day, and not just on days when Parliament is sitting. Three flags are used:

The Winter Union Flag, flown from September to April, measures 24 ft by 14 ft 4 in. (7.32m by 4.37m).

The Summer Union Flag is flown from April to September, but when the wind speed is more than 25mph the winter flag is used. The Summer Flag measures 36 ft by 18 ft (10.97m by 6.55m).

The Royal Standard is flown when Her Majesty the Queen is present in the Palace: on 20 March 2012, for the presentation of Loyal Addresses from the two Houses in Westminster Hall; on 9 May for the State Opening of Parliament; and on 5 June for the Jubilee Lunch given by the Livery of the City of London in Westminster Hall. The Victoria Tower Royal Standard measures 24 ft by 12 ft (7.32m by 3.65m).

Two other Union flags are flown every day: one on Portcullis House (12 ft by 7 ft 2 in., 3.66m by 2.18m); and one on the 1 Parliament Street building (8 ft by 4 ft 8 in., 2.44m by 1.42m).

In 2012 the Armed Forces Flag was flown on Portcullis House in the week leading up to Armed Forces Day; in honour of the London Olympic and Paralympic Games the Olympic Flag (the interlocking rings) was flown from 1 Parliament Street and Portcullis House during the Olympics. The Agitos Flag, symbol of the Paralympic Games, was similarly flown for those Games. (The Agitos Flag consists of three asymmetrical interlocking crescents of red, blue and green, the colours most widely used in national flags around the world.)

The flags are cared for and flown by the four Flagmen: Martin Lyford, Nigel Magnay, Michael King and Sunday Iyamu. The Victoria Tower is 323 feet (98.5m) high, and when it was built was the tallest secular building in the world: flying the flag from there in a stiff breeze requires good preparation and a head for heights!

BARRY AND SELECT COMMITTEES

I am in a towering rage and in the right humour for throwing up my appointment at the New Palace of Westminster, which I expect I shall be driven to do before long. All the arrangements of the new House of Commons, including the form, size, proportions, taste and everything else concerning it are in abeyance, and awaiting the fiat of a Committee of the House of Commons, of all tribunals the most unfit to decide.

Charles Barry, the architect of the Palace, to Augustus Welby Pugin, designer of the Palace's decoration, after an especially taxing session with the Building Committee, 1845

Charles Shaw Lefevre, Speaker from 1839 to 1857, was the last Speaker to be allowed to take away with him on retirement the splendid silver service provided by the government for banquets in Speaker's House.

WESTMINSTER BRIDGE

In the early eighteenth century the growing population of fashionable and wealthy Westminster led to pressure for a second Thames crossing. The City of London, jealous of Westminster's trade and economic standing, regarded a second crossing as the end of civilisation as then known but the pressure increased, and in 1721 '*divers Gentlemen, Freeholders, and Inhabitants of Westminster*' petitioned Parliament for a bridge across the Thames at the site of one of the horse ferries to Lambeth (the memory of which is preserved in the modern Horseferry Road) or at Vauxhall.

The Bill was brought in but aroused violent opposition. An anonymous pamphleteer summed it up:

The Birth-Right and Privileges of Freemen of London, will hereby in a little time become Contemptible: for as the South Sea has strip'd them of their superfluous Riches, long Wars, continued Taxes and high Duties, impair'd their Stock, and shock'd their Credit; so a new Bridge will take the Meat out of their Mouths, by drawing off their supply of Provisions, and pick the Money out of their Pockets, by enabling the Inhabitants of Westminster to trade at less Expences, Houses being at less Rents, Lodgers more frequent, and no Time or Money spent to qualify them for Shopkeepers... It will enrich the Inhabitants of Westminster, and impoverish the Citizens of London ... in short, it will make Westminster a fine City, and London a Desart...

The Bill was lost in 1722. But fourteen years later, in February 1736, the Burgesses, Freeholders and Inhabitants of Westminster again petitioned Parliament. The storm of opposition was renewed. It included the Archbishop of Canterbury, for whom the horse ferry from Lambeth to Westminster was a nice little earner. The City of London, ever apocalyptic, maintained that a second bridge (in competition with their own London Bridge) would make navigation of the Thames *'dangerous, if not impractical'*.

But the Westminster Bridge Act became law in 1736, and it opened the way for a complete remodelling of the surroundings of the Houses of Parliament. A narrow road to the river called Woolstaple was swept away, as was the Westminster Market, and Bridge Street took their place. To the north, White Horse Yard, Stephens Alley and Rhenish Wine Yard gave way to the wide and splendid Parliament Street; and Great George Street joined the new bridge to St James's Park, losing Thieving Lane in the process.

The new bridge, built of Portland stone, was opened on 18 November 1750. At 1,223 feet it was 300 feet longer than London Bridge. Surprisingly, it was designed by a Swiss, Charles Labelye – although he was a naturalised Briton.

A hundred years later the bridge was subsiding and in bad shape, and a new bridge was built. It was designed by Thomas Page and the Gothic detailing was by Sir Charles

Barry, the architect of the Palace of Westminster. The new bridge was opened on 24 May 1862.

A View of Westminster Bridge from Stangate Stairs,
John Boydell, 1755

Westminster Bridge, at the Commons end of the Palace, has green paintwork, the Commons colour. The Lords colour, red, is used for Lambeth Bridge, at the Lords end of the Palace.

KNOCKING

Ordered, that a Committee be appointed to inquire the causes of the late noises of knocking, that have been heard in the night in the Old Palace Yard and thereabouts, and to search the houses near the Houses of Parliament, and in the

Old Palace Yard, and to examine and return in the names of such Papists as inhabit near the two Houses of Parliament.
Journal of the House of Commons, 1 November 1678

THE POWER OF THE WHIPS

Maurice Edelman, Labour MP for Coventry North West, had a comfortable lifestyle and his Whips found that he was slightly less than biddable. In December 1975, with a tight vote on a three-line whip one night, Michael Cocks, the Labour Chief Whip, was told that Edelman might find it difficult to make the vote as he was giving an important dinner party at his Belgravia home. Cocks exploded. '*Snapey, go round to Edelman,*' he instructed his Whip colleague Peter Snape, '*and tell that bastard that if he isn't in the lobby tonight he's dead. Dead!*'

Snape got in a cab and delivered the message to Edelman, whom he found suave, dinner-jacketed and extremely unsympathetic. Snape delivered the Chief's message and left.

The government scraped through the vote. Later that night, as he was driving back to his West Bromwich constituency, Snape turned on the Radio 4 News at Midnight. He was electrified to hear '*The death has just been announced of the veteran Labour MP Maurice Edelman...*'

In a somewhat nervous state he got home, parked his car and was unlocking his front door when he heard the telephone in the hall. He rushed in. It was the Chief Whip. There was a two-word conversation: '*Snapey? Overkill.*'

PETITIONS

Petitions have been part of the parliamentary process since the very earliest days. Some trace the legislative process back to the practice of petitioning the king through Parliament; even to this day private legislation at Westminster (that is, local legislation) begins with a petition. In the nineteenth century, when the majority of the population had no right to vote, petitioning was one of the principal ways of bringing matters to the attention of Parliament.

1843 was the record year for the number of signatures on petitions – 6,135,050. Those were the signatures admitted as genuine; the Public Petitions Committee (abolished in 1974) often had to report, in sorrow or in anger, that petition signatures were false (it was unlikely that, for example, Queen Victoria or the Duke of Wellington spent much time signing petitions). The most petitions in a Session – 33,742 – were presented in 1892–93, but by 1919 the number had dropped to 121.

THE SOCIALIST ABC, BY ALEX GLASGOW

When that I was but a little tiny boy, me Daddy said to me,
'The time has come, me bonny, bonny bairn,
To learn your ABC'.
Now Daddy was a lodge chairman

In the coal fields of the Tyne;
And his ABC was different
From the Enid Blyton kind.

He sang 'A is for Alienation
That made me the man I am, and
B's for the Boss who's a Bastard,
A Bourgeois who don't give a damn.
C is for Capitalism,
The bosses' reactionary creed, and
D's for Dictatorship, laddie,
But the best proletarian breed.
E is for exploitation,
That workers have suffered so long, and
F is for old Ludwig Feuerbach,
The first one to say it was wrong.
G is for all Gerrymanderers,
Like Lord Muck and Sir Whatsisname, and H is the Hell that they'll go to,
When the workers have kindled the flame.
I's for Imperialism,
And America's kind is the worst, and
J is for sweet Jingoism,
That the Tories all think of the first.
K is for good old Keir Hardie,
Who fought out the working class fight, and
L is for Vladimir Lenin,
Who showed him the left was all right.

M is of course for Karl Marx,
The Daddy and the Mammy of them all, and
N is for Nationalisation –
Without it we'd crumble and fall.
O is for overproduction,
That capitalist economy brings, and
P is for all Private Property, the greatest of all of the sins.
Q's for the Quid Pro Quo,
We'll deal out so well and so soon, when
R for Revolution is shouted, and
The Red Flag becomes the top tune.
S is for Sad Stalinism,
That gave us all such a bad name, and
T is for Trotsky the hero,
Who had to take all of the blame.
U's for the Union of Workers,
The Union will stand to the end, and
V is for Vodka, yes, Vodka,
The vun drink that von't bring the bends.
W's for all Willing Workers,
And that's where the memory fades,
For X, Y and Z, my dear Daddy said,
Will be written on the street barricades.'

Now that I'm not a little tiny boy,
My Daddy says to me,
'Please try to forget the things I said,
Especially the ABC'.

18

> *For Daddy is no longer a union man,*
> *And he's had to change his plea.*
> *His alphabet is different now,*
> *Since they made him a Labour MP.*

Alex Glasgow (1935–2001), the wonderfully uncompromising singer/songwriter from Gateshead, wrote the songs and music for the successful musical plays *Close the Coalhouse Door* and *On Your Way, Riley* by Alan Plater, and the scripts for the TV drama *When the Boat Comes In*, of which he sang the theme song.

THINGS THAT COULD HAVE BEEN SAID RATHER BETTER

> *When your backs are to the wall, that's when you turn round and fight*
> John Major, Prime Minister 1990–97

> *Creating the Green Belt was a great Labour achievement – and we're going to build on it!*

> *We will reduce and probably eliminate the homeless by 2008.*
> John Prescott, Deputy Prime Minister, 1997–2007

THINGS YOU SHOULDN'T ASK...

...Jack Straw, in a hospital during an election campaign, to someone who seemed a little confused: '*Do you know who*

I am?' Confused One (now as sharp as a tack): *'No dear, but if you ask Matron she's certain to know.'*

UNDER-PERFORMANCE

The legacy of the Great Fire of London and the burgeoning population of the capital meant that churches were in short supply. A committee of the House of Commons reported in April 1711 that no more than one in three of the population was provided for. The House resolved to legislate to put this right, and Parliament passed the Fifty New Churches Act 1711. Unfortunately, only twelve churches were built, but they were some of the most splendid London buildings of the eighteenth century, employing the talents of Hawksmoor, Archer, James and Gibbs: Christ Church, Spitalfields; St George in the East; St Anne's, Limehouse; St Alphege's, Greenwich; St Paul's, Deptford; St John Horsleydown, Bermondsey; St Luke's, Old Street; St Mary Woolnoth; St George's, Bloomsbury; St John's, Smith Square; St George's, Hanover Square, and St Mary le Strand.

Politics is like a chicken coop, and those inside get to behave as if their little run were all the world.
John Buchan, *Greenmantle*, 1916

Being an MP is the sort of job all working-class parents want for their children – clean, indoors and no heavy lifting.
Diane Abbott, Labour MP for Hackney North and Stoke Newington 1987–

There is only one line to be adopted in opposition to all tricks; that is the steady straight line of duty, tempered by forbearance, levity, and good nature.

Arthur Wellesley, 1st Duke of Wellington (1769–1852)

There is danger from all men. The only maxim of a free government ought to be to trust no man living with power to endanger the public liberty.

John Adams (1735–1826), Second President of the United States

In politics the middle way is none at all.

John Adams

JOURNALISTS

What can we do with these sort of fellows? We have no power over them. God, for my part, I will have no communication with any of them.

The Duke of Wellington

FILTHY WESTMINSTER

The Filth, Sir, of some Parts of the Town, and the Inequality and Ruggedness of others, cannot but in the Eyes of Foreigners disgrace our Nation, and incline them to imagine us as a People, not only without Decency, but without Government, a Herd of Barbarians, or a Colony of Hottentots. The most

disgusting Part of the Character given by Travellers, of the most Savage Nations, is their Neglect of Cleanliness, of which, perhaps, no Part of the World affords more Proofs than the Streets of London; a City ... which abounds with such Heaps of Filth, as a Savage would look on with Amazement.

Lord Tyrconnel, in the House of Commons, 1741

Remember – more stories come out of the Palace of Westminster than any other building in the land.

Chris Moncrieff, veteran Lobby journalist

Ernest Bevin, Labour Foreign Secretary from 1945 to 1951, was preparing to go to Paris for an international conference. One of his private secretaries asked, '*Will Mrs Bevin be accompanying you, Foreign Secretary?*'

'*Of course not,*' Bevin replied. '*When you go to dinner at the Ritz you don't take an 'am sandwich, do you?*'

In March 2011, the Father of the House, Sir Peter Tapsell, asked William Hague, the Foreign Secretary:

In the context of the very important question of Iran, may I tell my right hon. Friend that in my memory, since the days of Ernest Bevin, I have never known a Foreign Secretary surrounded simultaneously by so many problems? I want to tell him how much I admire the coolness and efficiency with which he is dealing with them.

Mr Hague:

> *My right hon. Friend is always respected as one of the wisest*
> *Members of the House. The fact that his recollections go*
> *back as far as Ernest Bevin is an inspiration to us, and the*
> *conclusion he draws is an inspiration to me.*

Eric Moonman, MP for Billericay from 1966, lost his seat in 1970 but was elected for Basildon in 1974. His campaign slogan, seen on thousands of posters, was LAUNCH MOONMAN!

After his success in the 1974 General Election, a young couple came to see him, They had done a lot of work in his campaign, despite the wife being heavily pregnant. They came to pay him a real tribute. *'We've called our son after you, Mr Moonman,'* they announced. Moonman expressed his pleasure, especially as Eric was now becoming an unusual name. The couple were aghast. *'No, oh, no – we haven't called him Eric. We've called him Launch...'*

LIBERALS ARE A LABOUR-SAVING DEVICE
Graffito at the LSE during the Lib–Lab Pact in 1978

SOME NICKNAMES

H. H. Asquith	*The Sledgehammer; Squiffy; Perrier Jouet*
Stanley Baldwin	*The Ironmonger; Honest Stan; Bonzo; God;* to his wife, *Tiger*

Arthur Balfour	*The Lisping Hawthorn Bird, Bloody Balfour* and (a little oddly to modern ears) *Pretty Fanny*
Andrew Bonar Law	*The Unknown Prime Minister*
Lord Brougham	*Brougham; Wickedshifts; Beelzebub*
Edmund Burke	*The Dinner Bell*

(strange given Burke's reputation as an orator, but he was able to empty the Chamber of the Commons pretty effectively)

James Callaghan	*Sunny Jim*
Henry Campbell-Bannerman	*CB*
Neville Chamberlain	*The Coroner*
Earl of Derby	*Scorpion Stanley; The Rupert of Debate*
Benjamin Disraeli	*Dizzy*
Sir Alec Douglas-Home	*Baillie Vass*

(a *Private Eye* running joke following a miscaptioned photograph in a local paper)

William Ewart Gladstone	*The Grand Old Man; The People's William*
Edward Heath	*Grocer*
Michael Heseltine	*Tarzan, Hezza*
Geoffrey Howe	*Mogadon Man* (*Private Eye* again)
David Lloyd George	*The Goat* – coined by Sir Robert Chalmers, Permanent Secretary to the Treasury from 1911 (Lloyd

George was Chancellor of the Exchequer from 1908 to 1911). Also *The Welsh Wizard* and *The Man Who Won The War*

Field-Marshal Earl Kitchener of Khartoum, Secretary of State for War 1914–16, said during the First World War that he always tried to avoid sharing military secrets with the Cabinet *'because they will all tell their wives in bed, apart from Lloyd George, who will tell other people's wives'*.

Lord Goderich	*Snip* or *Goody*
Lord Godolphin	*Volpone*
Harold Macmillan	*Supermac (Mac the Knife* after the 'Night of the Long Knives' – the sacking of six members of his Cabinet in 1962)
Peter Mandelson	*The Prince of Darkness*
Lord Palmerston	*Lord Cupid; Lord Pumicestone; The Mongoose*
Robert Peel	*Orange Peel* (from his outspoken opposition to the Roman Catholic emancipation urged by George Canning
John Prescott	*Prezza, Two Jags*
Lord John Russell	*Finality Jack; The Widow's Mite*

(he was only 5 ft 4 ¾ in. tall (164.5cm) and weighed eight stone (50.8 kg))

Lord Sandwich	*Jeremy Twitcher* or *Twitcher*
Dennis Skinner	*The Beast of Bolsover*

Margaret Thatcher   *The Iron Lady*
or according to Norman St John-Stevas, Leader of the
House of Commons in Margaret Thatcher's Cabinet, *The
Leaderene* and *TINA* (*There Is No Alternative*)
The Duke of Wellington   *Beau; the Duke; the Iron Duke*
Harold Wilson   *Wislon* (another *Private
                                                  Eye* coinage)

Edmund Burke (1729–97) by James Northcote,
after Reynolds

In 1750, Abingdon Street, which runs along the west side of the Palace of Westminster into Parliament Square, was created by the widening of the existing and insalubrious Dirty Lane.

PROROGATION...

...marks the end of a parliamentary Session. These days five Lords Commissioners act on behalf of the Queen, rather than the monarch proroguing in person. The Commissioners instruct Black Rod to summon the Commons, who come to the Bar of the House of Lords to hear the Commission for proroguing Parliament read, and the Speech (a retrospective version of the Queen's Speech at the State Opening) read. Royal Assent is signified to the most recent Bills passed by the Clerk of the Parliaments saying of each one *La Reyne le veult.*

The occasion has changed little since the State Opening of 1663 described by Samuel Pepys, but it is rather better organised these days. In his diary entry for 27 July 1663 Pepys, who had spent the night at Epsom, describes coming back to London and spotting the King's Barge making ready to go to Westminster for the ceremony. Being Pepys, of course, he decides to follow the barge and gatecrash the ceremony:

> *...and so by water to Westminster and there came, most luckily, to the Lords' House as the House of Commons were*

going into the Lords' House, and there I crowded in along with the Speaker – and got to stand close behind him – where he made his speech to the King [a feature which has not survived to modern times].

The greatest matters were a Bill for the Lord's Day (which it seems the Lords have lost and so cannot be passed, at which the Commons are displeased) – the Bills against Conventicles and Papists (but it seems the Lords have not passed them); and giving His Majesty four entire subsidys.

In modern times only a few days elapse between proroga-tion and the next State Opening. Not so on 27 July 1663, when the King finished his speech by announcing that he *'for the better proceeding of Justice ... doth prorogue them to the 16th of March next'*.

HOUSE RULES

By a statute of Edward II, 1313, armour is not permitted to be worn in either House of Parliament.

REX V HADDOCK: IS IT A FREE COUNTRY?

In *Uncommon Law*, by A. P. Herbert, Albert Haddock, a man devoted (as was Herbert himself) to exposing the idiocies of the law, is arrested for jumping into the Thames from Hammersmith Bridge. When asked why he did it, he says 'for fun'.

The judge sums up:

*The appellant made the general answer that this was a free country and a man can do what he likes if he does nobody any harm. It cannot be too clearly understood that this is **not** a free country and it will be an evil day for the legal profession when it is ... and least of all may they do unusual actions 'for fun'. People must not do things for fun. There is no reference to fun in any Act of Parliament.*

(This case was strongly criticised in an American law journal, which failed to realise that it was *made up*.)

A man who has made up his mind on a given subject twenty-five years ago and who continues to hold his political opinions after he has been proved to be wrong is a man of principle; while he who from time to time adapts his opinions to the changing circumstances of life is an opportunist.

A. P. Herbert, in *Which is the Liberal Party?*

Lists of Acts given Royal Assent have a particular fascination. The short titles are ready to take wing as flights of fancy. One doesn't really want to be brought down to earth by what the statutes actually said. For example:

The Damaged Coffee etc. Act 1820; the Bringing of Coals etc. to London Act 1820; the Whipping Act 1820; the Discovery of Longitude at Sea etc. Act 1821; the Frauds by

Boatmen etc. Act 1821; the Cursing and Swearing Act 1823; the Bubble Companies etc. Act 1825; the Piratical Ships Act 1825; the Use of Fire on Steamboats Act 1828; the Cholera Prevention Act 1833; the Hanging in Chains Act 1834; the Tithing of Turnips Severed from the Ground Act 1835; the Offences Near The Cape of Good Hope Act 1836; the Act of Parliament (Mistaken References) Act 1837.

Sometimes there is a very modern resonance:

The Greek Loan Guarantee Act 1836.

FREE THE CHILTERN HUNDREDS

Anon., on a wall.

Does Magna Carta mean nothing to you? Did she die in vain?
Tony Hancock, *Hancock's Half-Hour*, 'Twelve Angry Men'

If there is no future life, this world is a bad joke – and whose joke?
A. J. Balfour

The Allied High Command have approached the Italian mainland like an old man approaching a young bride, fascinated, sluggish and apprehensive.
Aneurin Bevan, in the House of Commons, 1943

*In matters of commerce the fault of the Dutch,
Is offering too little and asking too much.*

The French are with equal advantage content,
So we clap on Dutch bottoms just twenty per cent.
George Canning, when Foreign Secretary, in a despatch to
Sir Charles Bagot, British Ambassador at The Hague

Save, oh save me from the candid friend.
George Canning

I wish I were as cocksure of anything as Tom Macaulay is
of everything.
Lord Melbourne

No man is regular in his attendance at the House of
Commons until he is married.
Benjamin Disraeli

A body of volunteers sent a document to William Pitt
offering themselves for military service, but hedging
the offer round with conditions and demands. One was
that they should never be required to leave England. Pitt
wrote in the margin:
Except in the case of actual invasion.

No Greek; as much Latin as you like; never French in any
circumstances; no English poet unless he has completed
his century.
Charles James Fox's advice on quotation in a House of
Commons debate

Burking Poor Old Mrs Constitution, Aged 141,
by William Heath, 1829

Sir Barnett Cocks, Clerk of the House of Commons 1962–
73, had two private secretaries: Miss Fox and Miss Pitt.

There are three golden rules for Parliamentary speakers:
Stand up. Speak up. Shut up.
James Lowther, Speaker of the House of Commons,
1905–21

Politics is the art of looking for trouble, finding it, misdiag-
nosing it, and then misapplying the wrong remedies.
Groucho Marx

Politics is perhaps the only profession for which no preparation is thought necessary.
Robert Louis Stevenson

He knows nothing and thinks he knows everything. That points clearly to a political career.
George Bernard Shaw

It is inexcusable for scientists to torture animals. Let them make their experiments on journalists and politicians.
Henrik Ibsen

In politics, never retreat, never retract, never admit a mistake.
Napoleon Bonaparte

Youth is a blunder; manhood a struggle; old age a regret.
Benjamin Disraeli

I'm an optimist; but an optimist who carries a raincoat.
Harold Wilson

A government that robs Peter to pay Paul can always rely on the support of Paul.
George Bernard Shaw

It is always the best policy to speak the truth – unless, of course, you are an exceptionally good liar.
Jerome K. Jerome

Speak when you are angry, and you will make the best speech you will ever regret.

Ambrose Bierce

Attributed to more than one MP in the now rather more distant past is the practice of writing back to any constituent on any subject whatsoever: *'Thank you very much for your letter. With people like you, England has nothing to fear.'*

Peace will come to earth when the people have more to do with each other and the government less.

Richard Cobden, MP 1841–57 and 1859–65

Cobden was a powerful advocate of free trade and its role in international peace and understanding. His crucial role in the repeal of the Corn Laws made him a controversial figure in the House, and Harriet Martineau recorded of his maiden speech on 24 August (!) 1841 that *'he was not treated in the House with the courtesy usually accorded to a new Member, and it was perceived that he did not need such observance'*.

I never see and converse with him without reproaching myself for the sort of hostility I feel towards his political conduct, for there are a simplicity, a gaiety and a natural urbanity and good-humour in him, which are remarkably captivating in so great a man.

Charles Greville of the Duke of Wellington, May 1832

In 1924, according to Evelyn Waugh's diary, a High Court judge presiding in a sodomy case and due to pronounce sentence the next morning asked F. E. Smith (by then Lord Birkenhead, and Lord Chancellor), *'What do you think you should give a man who allows himself to be buggered?'* Smith answered instantly, *'Oh, thirty shillings, or two pounds – whatever you happen to have on you.'*

Lord Liverpool was in office for all but thirteen months of his thirty-six years in Parliament – nearly fifteen of those years as Prime Minister. Lord Melbourne was in office continuously for forty-six years.

He has joined what even he would admit to be the majority.
John Sparrow, Warden of All Souls, Oxford, 1952–77, on the death of a proponent of proportional representation

An insular country, subject to fogs and with a powerful middle class, requires grave statesmen.
Benjamin Disraeli

A maiden speech so inaudible that it was doubted whether after all the young orator really did lose his virginity.
Benjamin Disraeli

Politics is the art of choosing between the disastrous and the unpalatable.
J. K. Galbraith

OXFORD V CAMBRIDGE

In Prime Ministers, Oxford wins 26 to 14.

The colleges score: Christ Church 13 (George Grenville, Shelburne, Portland, William Grenville, Liverpool, Canning, Peel, Derby, Gladstone, Salisbury, Rosebery, Eden, Douglas-Home); Trinity 3 (Wilmington, Pitt the Elder, North); Balliol 3 (Asquith, Macmillan, Heath); Brasenose 2 (Addington, Cameron); Hertford (at that time Hart Hall) 1 (Pelham); University College 1 (Attlee); Jesus 1 (Wilson); Somerville 1 (Thatcher); St John's 1 (Blair).

William Pulteney, 1st Earl of Bath (Christ Church) is thought by some to have been Prime Minister in 1746, but even they admit that trying to form an administration for '48 ¾ hours, seven minutes and eleven seconds' in the chaos following the mass resignation of Pelham's Ministry probably doesn't count.

THE LONGEST ACT IN THE PARLIAMENTARY ARCHIVES...

...is the Land Tax Act 1821, which lists some 65,000 Commissioners appointed under the Act and is 380 yards (348m) in length.

SLEEPERS IN CABINET

- The Duke of Grafton
- Lord Grenville

- The Duke of Portland
- Lord Hartington

...were all notorious in their day for going to sleep in Cabinet meetings.

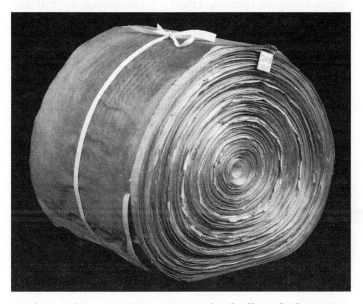

The Land Tax Act 1821, at 380 yards of vellum the longest Act in the Parliamentary Archives

The moving and seconding of the Humble Address of the Commons for the Queen's Speech at the start of a Session is traditionally done by a genial old codger on the way out and an oily young man on the way up.
Peter Lilley

Gladstone's speeches occupy 18,000 columns of Hansard, and appear in 366 volumes.

Sir, you are in a devilish awkward predicament, and must get out of it as best you can.
The Duke of Wellington, when asked for advice

All political lives, unless they are cut off in midstream at a happy juncture, end in failure, because that is the nature of politics and of human affairs.
Enoch Powell

ODD OFFICES

The Cofferer of the Household was an officer of state, and a member of the Privy Council and of the Board of Green Cloth. Under the Comptroller he had supervision of other Royal officials, and paid their wages.

The Board of Green Cloth audited the accounts of the Royal Household and sat as a court on offences committed on land of the Royal Palaces. It took its name from the green baize covering the table at which its meetings were held. In later years it dealt with liquor, betting and gaming licences for premises controlled by the Royal Palaces, and did not finally disappear until 2004, following the Licensing Act 2004.

The First Clerk of the Green Cloth (there were four Clerks or Clerk-Comptrollers) was Secretary of the Board of Green Cloth, and was responsible for organising

Royal journeys. It was a lucrative post: in the seventeenth century the Clerks received £500 a year (£64,000 today), plus fees, lodging and rights of '*Wast, Command and Remaines*' (leftover provisions). The latter was replaced by a further allowance of £518 in 1761, making a total of £1,018, or £130,000 in today's money. The Clerks of the Green Cloth were abolished in 1782.

The Lord Keeper of the Great Seal had physical custody of the Great Seal of England. The Seal, first used by Edward the Confessor, was normally in the hands of the Chancellor of England, but from Thomas à Becket's time the duty usually devolved upon a vice-chancellor. The status of the Lord Keeper was finally fixed by the Lord Keeper Act of 1562. The post of Lord Keeper was combined with that of Lord Chancellor in 1761, and the present Lord Chancellor and Secretary of State for Justice is responsible for the custody of the Great Seal.

SHORT OF CASH

In May 2010 the incoming Chief Secretary to the Treasury, Liberal Democrat David Laws, found on his desk a letter from his Labour predecessor, Liam Byrne. The letter said simply:

'Dear Chief Secretary, I'm afraid to tell you there's no money left. Kind regards and good luck.'

Laws said that this was '*honest but slightly less helpful advice than I had been expecting*'.

Byrne took a lot of stick for the gallows humour, but it was no more than the exchange eighty years before, when Winston Churchill greeted Philip Snowden, his successor as Chancellor of the Exchequer, on the steps of the Treasury with the news: '*Nothing in the till!*'

And Reggie Maudling, leaving office in 1964, left his successor as Chancellor of the Exchequer, James Callaghan, a note saying: '*Good luck, old cock ... Sorry to leave it in such a mess.*'

At a levee at Buckingham Palace in 1931 King George V asked Jimmy Thomas, Secretary of State for the Dominions and Secretary of State for the Colonies in Ramsay MacDonald's National government, whether the international financial situation was quite as bad as the Chancellor of the Exchequer, Philip Snowden, kept on telling him. Thomas said: '*Sir, it's that serious that if I was you I'd put the colonies in the wife's name.*'

Well, fancy giving money to the government!
Might as well have put it down the drain.
Fancy giving money to the government!
Nobody will see the stuff again.

Well, they've no idea what money's for;
Ten to one they'll start another war.
I've heard a lot of silly things, but

Lor', fancy giving money to the government.
A. P. Herbert

That is not just a legacy, it is there for the future.
Alex Salmond, First Minister of Scotland 2007–

*I have, alas, only one illusion left, and that is the Archbishop
of Canterbury.*
The Rev. Sydney Smith (1771–1845)

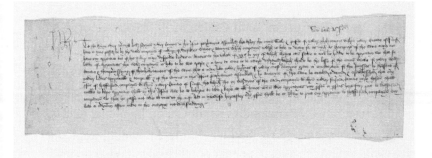

The oldest Act of Parliament kept at Westminster: *An Act
for taking of Apprentices to make Worsteds in the County
of Norfolk*, 1497

Mr Redwood: *To ask the Minister of State, Department
for Business, Innovation and Skills, whether EU Working
Time Directive restrictions on working hours apply to hon.
Members when (a) acting as constituency Members and (b)
undertaking duties in the House.*
Mr McFadden: *The regulations implementing the*

Working Time Directive in the UK apply to 'workers'. A 'worker' is someone who works under a contract of employment or a contract to perform personally any work or services for another party whose status is not that of a client or customer. Holders of political and elected office are not regarded as 'workers' and are therefore not covered by the regulations.

House of Commons, 21 July 2009

THE PARLIAMENT OF 1581

Mr Popham, when he was Speaker, and the Lower House had sat long, and done in effect nothing, coming one day to Queen Elizabeth, she said to him: *'Now, Mr Speaker, what hath passed in the Lower House?'* He answered: *'If it please Your Majesty, seven weeks.'*

Sir Francis Bacon

TACT

This Earle of Oxford [Edward de Vere, 17th Earl, 1550–1604], *making his low obeisance to Queen Elizabeth, happened to let a Fart, at which he was so abashed and ashamed that he went to Travell, 7 yeares. On his returne, the Queen welcomed him home, and sayd, 'My Lord, I had forgott the Fart.'*

John Aubrey, *Brief Lives*

Asquith's lucidity of style is a positive disadvantage when he has nothing to say.
A. J. Balfour

I must remind the right honourable Gentleman that a monologue is not a decision.
Clement Attlee to Winston Churchill

The best argument against democracy is a five-minute conversation with the average voter.
Winston Churchill

Everyone has a right to pronounce foreign words as he chooses.
Winston Churchill

'KBO (Keep Buggering On)'
A favourite instruction of Churchill's

There are two problems in my life. The political ones are insoluble and the economic ones are incomprehensible.
Sir Alec Douglas-Home

I am more or less happy when being praised, not very comfortable when being abused, but I have moments of uneasiness when I am being explained.
A. J. Balfour

It is often said that the Central Lobby in the House of Commons is the third easiest place in Europe to pick people up after Funland in Leicester Square and the arrival lounge at Rome airport.

Alan Clark, MP for Plymouth Sutton (Nancy Astor's constituency!) 1974–92 and for Kensington and Chelsea 1997–99

The days and weeks of screwed-up smiles and laboured courtesy, the mock geniality, the hearty shake of the filthy hand, the chuckling reply that must be made to the coarse joke, the loathsome, choking compliment that must be paid to the grimy wife and sluttish daughter, the indispensable flattery of the vilest religious prejudices, the wholesale deglutition of hypocritical pledge.

Lord Salisbury, who, it may be noted, actually had to do very little of this himself.

THE *SPITTING IMAGE* SALE...

...took place at Sotheby's in July 2000. Some of the hammer prices for the puppets were:

- Margaret Thatcher £11,224 (and 'angry' version £5,299; with Denis Thatcher £4,490)
- Norman Tebbit £4,858
- John and Norma Major £3,165
- Tony and Cherie Blair £3,128

English policy is to float lazily downstream, occasionally putting out a diplomatic boathook to avoid collisions.
Lord Salisbury

My idea of an agreeable person is a person who agrees with me.
Benjamin Disraeli

The county of Yorkshire, which contains near a million souls, sends two county members; and so does the county of Rutland, which contains not a hundredth part of that number. The town of Old Sarum, which contains not three houses, sends two members; and the town of Manchester, which contains upwards of sixty thousand souls, is not admitted to send any. Is there any principle in these things?
Thomas Paine, *Rights of Man*

Writing about politics is 40 per cent hard work, 40 per cent good judgement and 20 per cent having a nose for when something is about to happen (you can call it good luck). The three are linked. The more you talk to people, the better the chance you have to pick up new political developments and changes in mood. The two big risks in political journalism are a lack of proportion and a lack of detachment. The dangers are exaggeration and excessive partisanship. You need to be close, but not too close. All politicians spin, they always have. The tricky task is to weave your way

45

through the propaganda. The fun of political journalism is that you have a unique insight into how we are governed: government and opposition, ministers and civil servants. And most of the time it is cock-up, rather than conspiracy.
Peter Riddell, Director of the Institute for Government and formerly Chief Political Commentator, *The Times*

A QUESTION TOO MANY

Charles Kennedy, when campaigning as Leader of the Liberal Democrats, visited a hospital. With the television cameras looking on, he asked one patient how she was going to vote. '*Liberal Democrat,*' she said.

'*Excellent, excellent,*' he responded. '*And ... er ... what are you in for?*'

'*Brain surgery,*' she said.

When Charles I made Oxford his headquarters during the English Civil War it was not an unmixed blessing to the (Royalist) Fellows:

To give a further character of the Court, though they were neat and gay in their apparell, yet they were very nasty and beastly, leaving at their departure their excrements in every corner, in chimneys, studies, cole-houses, cellars. Rude, rough, whoremongers; vaine, empty, careless.
Anthony Wood (1632–95), Fellow of Merton

THE GOLDEN THREAD

Monarchy is not just a golden bauble on the top of a stone pyramid, but more like the golden thread running through an entire tapestry.

Harold Wilson

2012 was Her Majesty the Queen's Diamond Jubilee, and the Diamond Jubilee weekend in June was an occasion of national rejoicing. Earlier in the year, on 20 March, the Queen received Loyal Addresses from both Houses in Westminster Hall. In reply she said, in part:

This great institution has been at the heart of the country and the lives of our people throughout its history. As Parliamentarians you share with your forebears a fundamental role in the laws and decisions of your own age.

47

Parliament has survived as an unshakeable cornerstone of our constitution and our way of life.

History links monarchs and Parliament, a connecting thread from one period to the next. So in an era when the regular, worthy rhythm of life is less eye-catching than doing something extraordinary, I am reassured that I am merely the second Sovereign to celebrate a Diamond Jubilee.

As today, it was my privilege to address you during my Silver and Golden Jubilees. Many of you were present ten years ago and some of you will recall the occasion in 1977. Since my Accession, I have been a regular visitor to the Palace of Westminster, and, at the last count, have had the pleasurable duty of treating with twelve Prime Ministers...

...The happy relationship I have enjoyed with Parliament has extended well beyond the more than three and a half thousand Bills I have signed into law. I am therefore very touched by the magnificent gift before me, generously subscribed by many of you. Should this beautiful window cause just a little extra colour to shine down upon this ancient place, I should gladly settle for that.

We are reminded here of our past, of the continuity of our national story and the virtues of resilience, ingenuity and tolerance which have created it. I have been privileged to witness some of that history and, with the support of my family, rededicate myself to the service of this great country and its people now and in the years to come.

The '*magnificent gift*' was the Diamond Jubilee window,

designed and made by the British artist John Reyntiens. Made from 1,500 pieces of glass in gold, blue, green and red, it depicts the Royal Arms. On the occasion of the Loyal Addresses it was in a special frame at floor level in Westminster Hall, but will be placed high up in the three central panels of the North Window of the Hall, where originally stained glass of the Royal Arms was placed by Henry VIII.

The Diamond Jubilee Window, Westminster Hall, 2012

One hundred and fifteen years earlier, in 1897, Queen Victoria's Diamond Jubilee was celebrated. On 21 June the House of Commons debated a motion to present an Address of Congratulations. The Prime Minister was Lord Salisbury, so in the Commons the motion was moved by A. J. Balfour, the First Lord of the Treasury. Balfour was the last person to hold this office separately from that of Prime Minister; since then they have always been combined.

Hansard reported:

The First Lord of the Treasury (*Mr A. J. Balfour, Manchester, E.*), *rising amid loud cheering from all parts of the House, said: I think, Mr Speaker, it will be admitted that but very few words are required from me to justify the Motion of which notice appears on the Order Paper. We should but very ill-represent the country at large if we remained silent and dumb, or refused to take any part in the chorus of congratulation which is arising from every portion of this vast Empire upon the auspicious anniversary which we are approaching* ['Hear, hear!']...

Sir, it is true that the reign of Her Majesty has been a reign of unexampled length. It is also true that it has been a reign of unexampled prosperity. Yet, in celebrating this Jubilee, we are not ministering, I believe, to sentiments of national vanity or to vulgar feelings of national compla-cency, but we are really offering up from our hearts a homage to the great lady who rules over us [Great cheering]. *Sir, if you ask, or if any ask, what are the virtues which have called forth this demonstration, if anybody asks what are the claims to this national regard, I think the answer is not difficult to give. It is because, as the Queen is pre-eminent in station, so she has been pre-eminent in virtue.* ['Hear, hear!'] *It is because she has so well understood the difficult and delicate tasks which fall to a constitutional monarch to perform, that the constitution of this country has during her reign been able to adapt itself, without friction and without shock, to the varying needs of this great community. It is because through a long and laborious life she has been animated by a single view of public duty* ['Hear, hear!']. *It is because in her public life she has been an example to every Sovereign, and in her private life an example to every citizen.* ['Hear, hear!', and cheers.] *It is because she has shared our anxieties and shared our triumphs. It is because throughout she has been animated and inspired by our national ideals, that this nation, and this House as representing this nation, delight to do her honour* [Cheers]. *It is therefore, Sir, with an absolute confidence that these sentiments, however feebly expressed, are the sentiments common to all who hear me that I beg now to move, That an humble Address be presented to Her Majesty, to congratulate Her Majesty on the auspicious completion of the sixtieth year of her happy reign; and to assure Her Majesty that this House profoundly shares the great joy with which her people celebrate the longest, most prosperous, and the most illustrious reign in their history; joining with them in praying earnestly for the continuance during many years of Her Majesty's life and health* [The right hon. Gentleman resumed his seat amid loud cheers from all parts of the House].

But for all the cheering, the Address to Queen Victoria was debated in contentious circumstances very different from those in which the Address to Queen Elizabeth II was agreed. In 1897 most of the Irish Members voted against the motion, which was agreed to by 459 votes to 44. The motion that the Address should be presented by the whole House was also divided upon, 411 to 41.

But once that was settled the House turned to the vital matter of what its Members should wear...

Sir J. Fergusson (Manchester, NE): May I ask you, Mr Speaker, as a great difference of opinion exists in the House on the subject, what dress hon. Members are expected to wear on the occasion of this Address being presented? I should also like to ask you for your advice, and for the expression of your wish as to whether hon. Members should proceed to the Palace in carriages or on foot?

Mr Speaker: As it is more than thirty-six years since an Address was presented to Her Majesty by the whole House, perhaps it would be convenient if I were to refer to the two points raised by the right hon. Baronet's question. [Cheers.] As regards dress, I understand it is usual for Members to go to the Palace in morning dress, except that Privy Counsellors usually wear levee dress.

As regards the mode of arriving at the Palace, shortly after

Prayers I shall proceed through St Stephen's Hall to New Palace Yard, followed by hon. Members, and thence drive at a walking pace to Buckingham Palace. I believe it has been usual for the bulk of hon. Members to follow on foot. [Cheers.] *Those hon. Members, however, who wear levee dress frequently go in carriages. I may add that going on foot very materially facilitates ingress to and egress from the Palace...*

Queen Victoria's Golden Jubilee: Trafalgar Square,
21 June 1887

Two days later, on 23 June 1897, Addresses were presented in the Ballroom at Buckingham Palace by 500 MPs and 200 peers.

Scarlet and gold, azure and gold, purple and gold, emerald and gold, always a changing tumult of colours that seemed

to list and gleam with a light of their own, and always
blinding gold. No eye could bear more gorgeousness.
A spectator at Queen Victoria's Diamond Jubilee,
Tuesday, 22 June 1897

The streets were beautifully decorated, also the balconies of
the houses, with flowers, flags and draperies of every hue.
Queen Victoria's more prosaic record of the same day in
her diary

In 1897 the Father of the House was Charles Pelham
Villiers. Born in 1802, at Victoria's Diamond Jubilee he
was the only remaining Member who had sat in the House
of Commons during the reign of William IV – he had been
elected for Wolverhampton in 1835.

As Father of the House, Villiers gave Queen Victoria
his personal Jubilee gift of a parasol, dressed in Chantilly
lace. One hundred and fifteen years later, the Father of the
House, Sir Peter Tapsell, followed his example, but this time
the parasol was dressed in Nottingham lace, as he said, *'from*
the city that first sent me to this place fifty-three years ago.'

After the death of Prince Albert in 1861, Queen Victoria
opened Parliament in person only seven times during the
remaining forty years of her reign.

In celebration of Queen Victoria's Diamond Jubilee, Leeds
and Sheffield were given Lord Mayors, and Nottingham,
Bradford and Kingston-upon-Hull became cities.

Imagine if at this moment, instead of the Queen, we had a gentleman in evening clothes, probably from Moss Bros, with a white tie, going about everywhere, who had been elected by some deal made between the extreme Left and the extreme Right. Then we would all wait for the next one, another little man, who is it going to be? 'Give it to X, you know he's been such a bad Chancellor of the Exchequer, instead of getting rid of him, let's make him the next President.' Can you imagine it? I mean, it doesn't make sense. That would be the final destruction of colour and life and sense of the past in this country, wouldn't it?

Harold Macmillan

Shortly after the dissolution in 1614 of the 'Addled' Parliament (so called because it passed no Bills) James I talked with Sarmiento, the Spanish Ambassador. The King complained that: *the House of Commons was a body with no head; its five hundred members voted without rule or order amid cries, shouts and confusion. He was astonished that his predecessors had tolerated such an assembly, but he had found it in England upon his arrival and had not been able to do without it.*

THE KING'S SPEECH

The first King's Speech of the First World War took place at the State Opening on 11 November 1914. In a remarkably powerful Speech from the Throne, King George V said:

The energies and sympathies of My subjects in every part of the Empire are concentrated on the prosecution to a victorious issue of the War on which we are engaged. I have summoned you now in order that sharing, as I am aware you do, My conviction that this is a duty of paramount and supreme importance, you should take whatever steps are needed for its adequate discharge.

Since I last addressed you, the area of the War has been enlarged by the participation in the struggle of the Ottoman Empire. In conjunction with My Allies, and in spite of continuous and repeated provocations, we strove to preserve, in regard to Turkey, a friendly neutrality. Bad counsels, and alien influences, have driven her into a policy of wanton and defiant aggression, and a state of war now exists between us. My Mussulman subjects know well that a rupture with Turkey has been forced upon Me against My will, and I recognise with appreciation and gratitude the proofs which they have hastened to give, of their loyal devotion and support.

My Navy and Army continue, throughout the area of conflict, to maintain in full measure their glorious traditions. We watch and follow their steadfastness and valour with thankfulness and pride, and there is, throughout My Empire, a fixed determination to secure, at whatever sacrifice, the triumph of our arms, and the vindication of our cause.

Gentlemen of the House of Commons,

You will be asked to make due financial provision for the effective conduct of the War.

My Lords and Gentlemen,

The only measures which will be submitted to you, at this stage of the Session, are such as seem necessary to My advisers for the attainment of the great purpose upon which the efforts of the Empire are set.

I confidently commend them to your patriotism and loyalty, and I pray that the Almighty will give His blessing to your counsels.

One day Queen Victoria asked Disraeli what his real religion was. *'Madam,'* he said, *'I am the blank page between the Old Testament and the New.'*

James I said that *'a man wishing a new law should come with a halter round his neck; and if the law proved unacceptable the propounder should be hanged forthwith.'* This policy would no doubt lead to a sharp reduction in the number of Private Members' Bills.

GEORGE R.

His Majesty, being desirous that a better and more suitable accommodation should be made for the residence of the Queen, in case she shall survive his Majesty, and being willing that the Palace in which his Majesty now resides, lately known by the name of Buckingham House, and now called the Queen's House, may be settled for that purpose, in lieu of Somerset House, recommends to his faithful Commons to take the same into consideration and to make provision for settling the said Palace upon her Majesty and for appropriating Somerset House to such uses as shall be found most beneficial for the people.

Journal of the House of Commons, 12 April 1775

BAGEHOTISMS

The Queen ... must sign her own death-warrant if the two Houses unanimously send it up to her.

Above all things our royalty is to be reverenced, and if you begin to poke about it you cannot reverence it... Its mystery is its life. We must not let in daylight upon magic.

The Sovereign has, under a constitutional monarchy such as ours, three rights – the right to be consulted, the right to encourage, and the right to warn.

Walter Bagehot, *The English Constitution,* 1867

The whole Constitution has been erected on the assumption that the King not only is capable of doing wrong but is more likely to do wrong than other men if he is given the chance.

A. P. Herbert, in *What is the Crown?*

HANDLING THE SOVEREIGN

I make it a rule never to interrupt him, and when in this way he tries to get rid of a subject in the way of business which he does not like, I let him talk himself out, and then quietly put before him the matter in question, so that he cannot escape from it.

The Duke of Wellington as Prime Minister, dealing with George IV, 1829

Weeding by the Head Gardener: the Duke of Wellington and George IV

Nancy Astor, on being invited by Edward VII to play cards: '*Cards, Sir? Why, I don't know the difference between a King and a knave.*'

Disraeli told Lord Esher (Lieutenant-Governor of Windsor Castle, and a confidant of Queen Victoria) that, in talking to the Queen, he observed a simple rule: '*I never deny. I never contradict... I sometimes forget.*'

In conversation with Matthew Arnold, Disraeli said: '*You have heard me accused of being a flatterer. It is true. I am a flatterer. I have found it useful. Everyone likes flattery, and when it comes to Royalty you should lay it on with a trowel.*'

Queen Victoria proroguing Parliament, House of Lords, 1851

Queen Victoria got on well with Disraeli, especially when he proposed the particularly grand flattery of giving her the title Empress of India. First impressions were promising. The Queen wrote in her diary shortly after Disraeli's appointment: *'The present man will do well, and will be particularly loyal and anxious to please me in every way. He is vy. peculiar, but vy. clever and sensible and vy. conciliatory.'*

The Act of Attainder (in effect, conviction for treason without the bother of a trial) of Queen Katherine Howard, 11 February 1542

Be not dismayed with the controlments and amendments of such things which you shall have done ... avoid opinion of being newfangled, a bringer-in of new customs.

Robert Beale, the Clerk of Queen Elizabeth I's Council, in his handover notes to his successor

When he has wearied me for two hours, he looks at his watch to see if he may not tire me for an hour more.

George III of Lord Grenville when Prime Minister

When the famously laconic Attlee went to Buckingham Palace to be asked to form an administration following the 1945 General Election, he is supposed to have spent some awkward moments with the King, also not given to garrulity. Finally Attlee said:

'*I've won the Election, Sir.*'

After a moment King George VI responded: '*Yes. I know. I heard it on the six o'clock news.*'

THE SARTORIAL

Lord Salisbury (3rd Marquess of Salisbury, three times Prime Minister between 1885 and 1902) once told his nursemaid that he wished he had been born a cat as he would not have had to change his clothes. Nothing if not consistent, he maintained this fine disregard for appearance throughout his life. Sir Frederick Ponsonby said that he had 'such ill-fitting breeches that they looked like ordinary trousers'.

As Prime Minister he was once refused admittance to a casino in Monte Carlo for being *unsuitably attired* – something that gave endless amusement to his irreverent family.

During a grave international crisis the Prince of Wales expressed his displeasure that Salisbury was wearing the trousers of an Elder Brother of Trinity House with the coat of a Civil Privy Counsellor (itself quite a sharp sartorial observation). Salisbury said that his valet was away; the Prince said that Salisbury should have noticed the solecism himself. Salisbury responded: *'I am afraid that at that moment my mind must have been occupied by some subject of less importance.'*

'Whist!'
The Duke of Wellington playing whist with Queen Victoria, 1839

Sir Frederick Ponsonby, Equerry-in-Ordinary to Queen Victoria 1894–1901, and Assistant Private Secretary both to Queen Victoria and Edward VII 1897–1910, wrote a frank autobiography *Recollections of Three Reigns*, not at all the sort of thing expected of a courtier. Nancy Mitford wrote to Evelyn Waugh saying that there was '*a shriek on every page*'.

If the King asks you to form a Government you say 'Yes' or 'No', not 'I'll let you know later'.
Clement Attlee

Lord John Townshend told me he had always foreseen the Coalition Ministry could not last, for he was at Court when Mr Fox kissed hands, and he observed George III turn back his eyes and ears just like a horse ... when the rider he has determined to throw is getting on him.
Lord John Russell

RED BOXES AND RESHUFFLES

His Majesty has thought proper to order a new commission of Treasury to be made out, in which I do not see your name.
Lord North to Charles James Fox, 24 February 1774

The red despatch box is a badge of ministerial office, but can also be a symbol of ministerial drudgery. *'Doing one's boxes' – getting through the mountain of ministerial home-work – means many a late evening or lost weekend.*

The red boxes are made of stained ram's leather, on a pine frame. They are lined with black satin – some with lead also, originally intended to ensure that a box would sink if thrown overboard. The lock is on the bottom, not the top, which is intended to ensure that the box is locked before it is carried. A minister leaving office usually has the perk of taking a box back to life as a backbencher.

There is a 'travel version' of the despatch box, in black so that it is less conspicuous.

CABINET-MAKING

Gladstone said that *'every Prime Minister has to be a good butcher'*.

Asquith, contemplating a reshuffle, repeated the observation, adding *'and there are several who must be pole-axed now'*.

He might make an adequate Lord Mayor of Birmingham – in a lean year.
Lloyd George about Neville Chamberlain

UNAVAILABLE

Sir Charles Dilke, tipped as a future Prime Minister, was ruined by a divorce case in 1886, in which it was alleged that he had seduced Virginia Eustace Smith shortly after her marriage to Donald Crawford MP (he had earlier certainly seduced Virginia's mother). The divorce was granted, and the rumour mill went to work on Dilke, not least giving him the nickname 'Three-in-a-Bed Dilke' because he was said to have invited a maidservant to join him and his mistress.

Gladstone ended Dilke's ministerial career by writing one word against his name in the Cabinet list: *'Unavailable'*. Dilke lost his Chelsea seat in the 1886 General Election, but sat as MP for the Forest of Dean 1892–1911.

The People's William (W. E. Gladstone),
by Spy, *Vanity Fair,* 1 July 1879

After Gladstone had sacked Dilke, he wrote him this letter, in its way magnificently Gladstonian:

My Dear Dilke,

I write to you, on this the first day of my going regularly to my arduous work, to express my profound regret that any circumstances of the moment should deprive me of the opportunity and hope of enlisting on behalf of a new Government the great capacity which you have proved in a variety of spheres and forms for rendering good and great service to Crown and country.

You will well understand how absolutely recognition on my part of an external barrier is separate from any want of inward confidence, the last idea I should wish to convey.

How can I close without fervently expressing to you my desire that there may be reserved for you a long and honourable career of public distinction?

Believe me always

Yours sincerely

W. E. Gladstone

THE STYLES OF PALMERSTON AND GLADSTONE COMPARED

Suppose the Prime Minister and the Chancellor of the Exchequer were each to be asked what day the Session would be over. Lord Palmerston would reply that it was the intention of Her Majesty to close the Session on the 18th of August.

Mr Gladstone would possibly premise that inasmuch as it was for Her Majesty to decide upon the day which would be most acceptable to herself, it was scarcely compatible with Parliamentary etiquette to ask her ministers to anticipate such decision; but presuming that he quite understood the purport of the Right Honourable Gentleman's question, of which he was not entirely assured, the completion of the duties of the House of Commons, and the formal termination of the sitting of the Legislature, being two distinct things, he would say that Her Majesty's ministers had represented to the Queen that the former would probably be accomplished about the 18th of August, and that such day would not be unfavourable for the latter, and, therefore, if the Sovereign should be pleased to ratify that view of the case, the day that he had named would very likely prove to be that enquired after by the Right Honourable Gentleman.

Quarterly Review, 1855

OF ONE OF MARGARET THATCHER'S CABINETS:

If they'd all been born in the same village, you'd be testing the water.

Anonymous

More Estonians than Etonians

Harold Macmillan

PLUS ÇA CHANGE

The position of junior Ministers today is not happy. They have responsibility for decisions, the reasons for which they do not know. They seldom have any effective voice in policy. On the other hand most [governments] *today contain half a dozen Cabinet Ministers who are there for past services or for other reasons unconnected with their present suitability for the positions which they occupy. Some of them are generally too old and out of date.*

Among the junior ministers will be found at least half a

dozen who are capable of original work, and of giving a lead. They are young and more in touch with the needs of the age.
Clement Attlee

Minister for Folding Deckchairs.
Chris Mullin, a junior minister in three departments 1999–2005, of himself

As a Parliamentary Secretary, the lowest rank of minister, Mullin once received an invitation which had been sent to his superior, the Minister of State, Nick Raynsford. Unfortunately Raynsford's Private Secretary's note was still attached: *'This is very low priority. I suggest we pass it to Chris Mullin.'*

I do not recall ever being given any indication of what was expected of me on being appointed to any political job.
Michael Heseltine

[We] have done nothing to lower the expectations of the public which are now very, very much higher than they used to be and governments do not deny that they can cure every ill that society suffers from ... this leads to an infantilisation of the public who are led to believe that any problem they face is the fault of their political masters, who shall be expected to sort it out within the next two or three weeks. This gives a breathlessness to government which is not very good.
Kenneth Clarke, Lord Chancellor and Secretary of State

for Justice (and a former Chancellor of the Exchequer and Home Secretary, who was a minister throughout the period 1979–97), giving evidence to the Commons Public Administration Select Committee

PURPOSEFUL CALM

An air of purposeful calm usually gets results. Throwing tantrums gets people scurrying around, but it also causes fear and stress, and fear and stress tend to lead to bad briefing and poor decisions.

National School for Government, *Handbook for Ministers*

The first forty-eight hours decide whether a minister is going to run his office or whether it is going to run him.

Arthur Henderson (1863–1935) the first Labour Cabinet Minister (President of the Board of Education in Asquith's 1915 coalition government)

I have never worked among a group of people who disliked and distrusted each other as much.

Richard Marsh (1928–2011), Minister of Power and Minister of Transport 1966–69, of the 1964 Wilson Cabinet

Marsh once described socialism as '*more people being able to enjoy smoked salmon*'. After several dozen functions at which he was served smoked salmon he also let it be known that he liked veal.

Between 1947 and 1997 the average length of time in a ministerial job was:

- 26.8 months for junior ministers
- 27.2 months for ministers of state
- 28 months for cabinet ministers

The Crown is, according to the saying, 'the fountain of honour', but the Treasury is the spring of business.
Walter Bagehot, *The English Constitution*, 1867

CLASSIC SYMPTOMS OF PRIVATE OFFICE DYSFUNCTIONALITY

- Abrupt departures of private secretaries
- The minister acquires the reputation of being difficult
- Appalling morale in private office
- Rumours circulate about tantrums and fights
- Inability to recruit leading to a series of temps in key jobs
- Regular cock-ups due to lack of institutional memory and disinclination to go the extra mile for the minister

National School for Government, *Handbook for Ministers*

It requires a great deal of time to have opinions. Our system, indeed, seems expressly provided to make it unlikely.
Walter Bagehot

Iron railings leaning out of the perpendicular.
Palmerston's description of Foreign Office handwriting

Benjamin Franklin was Clerk of the Pennsylvania Assembly when it was suggested that he might become a Member of the Assembly:

The latter station was the more agreeable to me, as I was at length tired with sitting there to hear debates in which as Clerk I could take no part, and which were often so unentertaining, that I was induc'd to amuse myself with making magic Squares, or Circles, or anything to avoid weariness. And I conceiv'd my becoming a Member would enlarge my power for doing Good.

Later he recorded: '*On taking my seat in the House, my Son was appointed their Clerk.*'

At a Whig election strategy meeting in 1859 there was a suggestion that they should use publicly the allegation that the 75-year-old Lord Palmerston had fathered an illegitimate child. '*Good God, no!*' exclaimed another: '*if that gets out he'll sweep the country!*'

On 11 August 2011, during the recall of Parliament, David Cameron made a statement on public order following widespread unrest and looting. The statement and the questions which followed lasted for two hours and forty-five minutes, and the Prime Minister replied to supplementary questions from 160 Members – certainly a record.

IDENTIKIT OF AN IDEAL MINISTER

- Sets clear goals
- Makes decisions; has good judgement
- Prepares and prioritises
- Listens
- Can learn quickly from experience
- Has personal resilience and stamina
- Copes well and maintains good relationships under pressure
- Knows how to motivate ministers, civil servants and to use a department
- Has authority within government and externally with Parliament, the media and the public
- Achieves objectives for change

Institute for Government

On 2 May 1997 I walked into No. 10 Downing Street as PM for the first time. I had never held office, not even as the most junior of junior ministers. It was my first and only job in government.
Tony Blair

Reforming the Civil Service is like drawing a knife through a bowl of marbles
Anonymous

The business of the Civil Service is the orderly management of decline.

Sir William Armstrong, Head of the Home Civil Service, 1968–74

It is an inevitable defect, that bureaucrats will care more for routine than results ... a bureaucracy is sure to think that its duty is to augment official power, official business, or official members, rather than to leave free the energies of mankind; it overdoes the quantity of government, as well as impairs its quality.

Walter Bagehot, *The English Constitution,* 1867

I used to check up to make sure that Cabinet decisions were carried out, but I soon realised it wasn't necessary. The civil servants came out of their caves, like hungry animals, and gobbled them up.

R. A. Butler, variously Deputy Prime Minister, Foreign Secretary, Home Secretary and Chancellor of the Exchequer, 1951–64

The first requirement of politics is not intellect or stamina but patience. Politics is a very long-run game and the tortoise will usually beat the hare.

John Major

THE WHO? WHO? MINISTRY

Lord Derby's first Conservative administration replaced

Lord John Russell's Whig government in February 1852, but lasted only until December that year. Its members had little experience (although it had rising stars in Salisbury and Disraeli). It was burdened with this nickname on the first day: as the members of the Cabinet were being read out in the House of Lords, the very deaf Duke of Wellington (then in the last months of his life) said loudly of each one: '*Who? Who?*'

THE MINISTRY OF ALL THE TALENTS...

...was a cross-party coalition formed by Lord Grenville in February 1806 after the death of William Pitt the Younger. With the country at war Grenville aimed at the strongest team available, regardless of party – and its inclusiveness was demonstrated by the appointment of Charles James Fox as Foreign Secretary and Leader of the House of Commons. The Grenville Ministry lasted for only just over a year; it failed to bring an end to the war, but did outlaw the slave trade before foundering on the question of Roman Catholic emancipation.

THE SACK

A junior minister was summoned to No. 10 to see Attlee. Cheerfully expecting some praise for his work, he asked the Prime Minister what he could do for him. '*I want your job,*' said Attlee.

'*But ... but, why, Prime Minister?*'
'*Afraid you're not up to it.*'

No more was said.

It's passed on, like a Christmas tree, from person to person.
John Prescott

It's not a referendum any more, it's a choice.
Gordon Brown

The European Parliament seems to be a place where the politicians go to milk the gravy train.
BBC World Service

The best way I know to win an argument is to start by being in the right.
Quintin Hogg (later Lord Hailsham)

The intelligent are to the intelligentsia what a gentleman is to a gent.
Stanley Baldwin

HECKLING...

...originally meant to tease or comb out fibres of flax or hemp. The political meaning probably came from radical Dundee in the early nineteenth century, where the hecklers who combed the flax were especially belligerent.

Alas, '*heckling*' has come to be used simply of interruptions or shouted insults, but it needs some wit (ideally on both sides), not just noise.

An all-purpose response to the serial interrupter: *'Your bus goes in five minutes. Be under it.'*

A Long Headed Election, by George Moutard Woodward; an eighteenth-century election

Quintin Hogg, later Lord Hailsham, had a direct and unsubtle way with hecklers. In the 1964 election campaign, assailed at a public meeting by a long-haired opponent, he responded: *'Now see here, Sir or Madam, whichever the case may be, we have had enough of you.'* On another occasion someone in the crowd waved a Harold Wilson poster at him. Hogg attacked it with his walking stick – an enduring television image.

Campaigning in the south-west, Quintin Hogg was

accused by someone at the back of the hall of vote-catching. '*Of course I am, you bloody fool,*' Hogg responded. '*Why else do you think I am speaking at an election meeting?*'

A hardy perennial, an example of which is Harold Wilson electioneering in Chatham, speaking warmly of the town and all that Labour policies would do for it.

Wilson: '*And why am I saying this?*'

A voice: '*Because you're in Chatham!*'

Heckler, trying to make something of Nancy Astor's metropolitan outlook:

'*Here, missus, how many toes are there on a pig's foot?*'

Nancy Astor: '*Take off your boots, man, and count for yourself.*'

Churchill, on a lecture tour in the US, to an angry anti-colonialist:

AA-C: '*What are you going to do about the Indians?*'

Churchill: '*Whose Indians – yours or ours?*'

Jimmy Maxton, electioneering in Glasgow, a messianic figure with hair down to his shoulders: '*Just think, in the British islands there are now three million people unemployed.*'

Voice from the crowd: '*And half of them are barbers!*'

Nancy Astor and an Irish heckler at an election meeting in the Plymouth Sutton constituency:

'Go back to America!'

'Go back to Lancashire, you don't belong in Plymouth.'

'I'm an Irishman.'

'I knew it! I knew you were an imported interrupter.'

'If I imported you, I'd drown myself in the sea.'

'More likely in drink.'

'I don't drink.'

'Well, go and have a drink today – it might sweeten you.'

That was when you were only a worried look on your father's face.

Response to any heckler's reference to the past

The Election: the New Member Addresses the People,
by C. F. Wicksteed, 1838

THE HOUSE OF LORDS

❧

If a second Chamber dissents from the first Chamber, it is mischievous; if it agrees, it is superfluous.
Emmanuel Joseph Sieyès (Abbé Sieyès) (1748–1836), constitutional drafter in revolutionary France

⁂

PERFECT PITCH

Lord German: *Can we identify where the very annoying F# is coming from in this Room and distracting me? I wonder whether it is possible to identify where it is and stop it.*
The Deputy Speaker (Lord Haskel): *It comes from the circulation of the air. I have been in here before when it has happened. I think the engineer knows how to fix it.*
House of Lords, Grand Committee Room, 20 October 2011

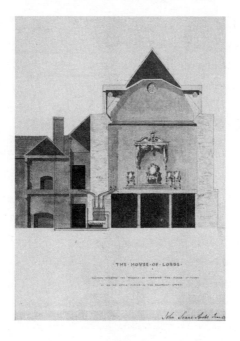

Sir John Soane's Plan for Warming and Ventilating the House of Lords, 1794

We know the House of Peers have made noble stands, when the House of Commons durst not. The last two years of [a] Parliament they dare not contradict the populace.
Samuel Johnson, reported by James Boswell in *The Journal of a Tour to the Hebrides*, entry for 24 August 1773

PEERS' TEST MATCH BATTING AVERAGES

- 7th Lord Hawke: 7.85
- Lord Constantine: 19.24

- 4th Lord Harris: 29.00
- Rt Rev. Lord Sheppard of Liverpool: 37.8
- Lord Cowdrey of Tonbridge: 44.06
- Baroness Heyhoe-Flint: 45.54

From Lords Hansard, 23 May 2011

Foreign and Commonwealth Office: Library

Asked by **Lord Jay of Ewelme**

To ask Her Majesty's Government what their plans are for the future of the stuffed anaconda in the Foreign and Commonwealth Office library.

The Minister of State, Foreign and Commonwealth Office (Lord Howell of Guildford): *Albert, the 20-foot long stuffed anaconda, has graced the Foreign and Commonwealth Office (FCO) library for over a century. He remains proudly in place, just as he did throughout the noble Lord's distinguished career in the FCO, and continues to be held in great affection by FCO staff. We have no plans for Albert other than to clean and stuff him from time to time.*

I wouldn't like to go to a dentist who, just before he drilled my teeth, told me he was not a dentist himself but that his father had been a very good dentist.

Tony Benn, on hereditary peers

PEERS ONLY

Sign on certain lavatories in the House of Lords

Asked by **Lord Berkeley**

To ask Her Majesty's Government why they transported a military band to the Falkland Islands to celebrate the Queen's Birthday on 21st April after their musical instruments were removed before take-off; what contribution the band was able to make to the celebrations without any instruments; and what were the costs of such personnel transport to and from the United Kingdom.

The Parliamentary Under-Secretary of State, Ministry of Defence (Lord Astor of Hever): *Members of the military band of the 4th Battalion The Mercian Regiment travelled to the Falkland Islands on 16th April. The band's instruments were classified as freight rather than passenger hold baggage and in error were not loaded on to the flight, the hold of which was full to capacity with other essential freight. The next flight to the Falkland Islands did not depart until 23rd April, so the personnel were unable to participate as planned in The Queen's Birthday Parade. Instead they undertook a programme of familiarisation and training with British Forces South Atlantic Islands. The personnel travelled using spare capacity on the Ministry of Defence's South Atlantic Airbridge. This represented no extra cost to the Department, other than the air passenger duty for the band's seats which amounted to a maximum of £2,040.*

From Lords Hansard, 13 May 2011

80% OF BISHOPS TAKE *THE TIMES*

Poster, amended by passer-by: THE OTHER 20% BUY IT

COMITY...

...is the term used for the relations of mutual respect between Commons and Lords. Over the years mutual respect has been able to accommodate trenchant criticism:

In 1880 Henry Labouchere tried to table a motion for debate in the same terms as that tabled and debated in the Long Parliament: *'That the House of Lords is useless and dangerous, and ought to be abolished.'* Despite the powerful historical precedent, Speaker Brand would not allow 'useless' but did allow 'dangerous'.

In the Commons debate on second reading of the Parliament Bill in 1910 one Member said:

It is certainly discouraging to an admirer of the heredi-tary system to take note of the mental calibre, not to say the physical appearance, of certain noble lords who are dug up from their graves of dignified oblivion to assist in defeating a measure which is distasteful to the hereditary Chamber.

Although you cannot make a disorderly remark orderly by simply attributing it to someone else, Speaker Lowther may not have intervened in this case because the words were a quotation from the Duke of Marlborough.

The two Archbishops and the Bishop of Durham hold their

office '*by Divine Providence*' all the other Bishops hold theirs '*by Divine Permission*'. Hensley Henson, Bishop of Hereford and then of Durham 1917–39, asserted that some Bishops hold their office '*by Divine Inadvertence*'.

BELLS

[of the placing of an amendment to a Bill:] *it offers late rather than early assistance in illuminating the first four lines of that page. It is the opposite of the example once set by a Polish Bishop who was visiting a parish in his diocese, an episode that could be helpful to many a parliamentarian. When greeted by the curate, the Bishop said, 'When I visit parishes in my diocese, I am accustomed to be greeted by the sound of bells, and that has not happened today'. The curate said, 'My Lord, there are three reasons. The first is that there are no bells'. 'Pray go no further' said the Bishop.*

Lord Brooke of Sutton Mandeville, House of Lords, 5 July 2011

LORDS REFORM

Iolanthe was the seventh Gilbert and Sullivan opera, and one of the most successful (the name was changed to *Iolanthe* from *Perola* less than a fortnight before the opening performance). It was the first to be produced at the Savoy Theatre, opening there on 25 November 1882 for an initial run of 398 performances.

Enter Lord Mountararat and Lord Tolloller from Westminster Hall:

CELIA (A FAIRY): *You seem annoyed.*

MOUNTARARAT: *Annoyed? I should think so! Why, this ridiculous protégé of yours* [Strephon, Arcadian shepherd, half-man, half-immortal, for whom the Queen of the Fairies has found a safe seat] *is playing the deuce with everything! Tonight is the Second Reading of his Bill to throw the Peerage open to competitive examination!*

TOLLOLLER: *And he'll carry it, too.*

MOUNTARARAT: *Carry it? Of course he will. He's a Parliamentary Pickford – he carries everything!*

LEILA (A FAIRY): *Yes. If you please, that's our fault.*

MOUNTARARAT: *The deuce it is!*

CELIA: *Yes; we influence the Members, and compel them to vote just as he wishes them to.*

LEILA: *It's our system. It shortens the debates.*

MOUNTARARAT: *Well, but think what it all means. I don't so much mind for myself, but with a House of Peers with no grandfathers worth mentioning, the country must go to the dogs!*

LEILA: *I suppose it must.*

MOUNTARARAT: *I don't want to say a word against brains – I've a great respect for brains – I often wish I had some myself – but with a House of Peers composed exclusively of people of intellect, what's to become of the House of Commons?*

LEILA: *I never thought of that.*

MOUNTARARAT: *This comes of women interfering in politics. It so happens that if there is an institution in Great Britain which is not susceptible of any improvement at all, it is the House of Peers!*
W. S. Gilbert, 1882

*The House of Lords **should** be an irrationally constituted body, like a jury.*
Sir Donald Somervell, Attorney General 1936–45

The Archbishop of Canterbury was on the Council of the Board of Trade until 1882, received notices of meetings until 1911, and was long thereafter invited to the annual dinner.

The Lord Bishop of Bath and Wells: *My Lords, there is a story of a man being audited by a tax inspector. 'How have you managed to buy such a luxurious villa when your income is so low?' asks the inspector. 'It's like this,' replies the man, 'While I was fishing last summer I caught a large golden fish. When I took it off the hook, the fish opened its mouth and said "I am a magical fish. Throw me back into the sea and I will give you the most luxurious villa you have ever seen". So I threw the fish back into the sea and got the villa.' The tax inspector was not impressed. 'How do you expect to prove such a ludicrous story?' he asked. 'Well', the man replied, 'you can see the villa, can't you?'*
House of Lords, 4 November 2010

MISTAKEN IDENTITY

House of Lords Grand Committee, 17 November 2010

Baroness Quin: *In the consultations, did any of the responses raise some of the concerns that have been raised so interestingly today by the noble Lord, Lord Demon?*

Lord Henley: *'Demon'?*

Baroness Quin: *I think I said 'Demon'.*

Lord Henley: *It is the noble Lord, Lord Deben. I think the noble Lord, Lord Demon, might be someone rather different. However, that might be for another life of my noble friend.*

Lord Deben: *I hope not.*

[The former John Selwyn Gummer, created Lord Deben in 2010.]

No reference to mistaken identity should omit the Duke of Wellington, accosted in the street:

'*Mr Jones, I believe?*'

The Duke: '*If you will believe that, you will believe anything.*'

The 'Mr Jones' was George Jones, RA, the painter and Secretary of the Royal Academy, who rather liked being taken for the Duke. When told about this, Wellington said: '*Mistaken for me, is he? That's strange, for no one ever mistakes me for Mr Jones.*'

HOUSE OF LORDS

Die Jovis 3 Februarii 1977

MINUTES OF PROCEEDINGS

PRAYERS – Read by the Lord Bishop of Worcester

Marquessate of Donegall – Report made by the Lord Chancellor that Dermot Richard Claud Marquess of Donegall has established his claim to the Marquessate of Donegall; and ordered to lie upon the Table.

NEW PEERS

Created on the recommendation of :

Tony Blair 1997–2007: Conservative, 62; Labour, 162; Lib Dem, 54; Independent/Crossbench/other, 96. Total 374.

Gordon Brown 2007–10: Conservative, 4; Labour, 11; Lib Dem, 2; Independent/Crossbench/other, 17. Total 34.

David Cameron 2010 up until June 2012: Conservative, 47; Labour, 39; Lib Dem, 24; Independent/Crossbench/other, 10. Total 120.

Total 1997–2012: 528, or 33 a year.

PROBLEMS OF ETIQUETTE

Lord Phillips of Sudbury: ...*Those who have added their names to the amendment and, at an earlier stage, Earl Erroll –*
Earl Ferrers: *Of.*
Lord Phillips of Sudbury: *I beg your pardon.*

Earl Ferrers: *My noble friend referred to Earl Erroll. Actually, he should have said the noble Earl, Lord Erroll, but if he was going to say Earl Erroll, he ought to have said the Earl of Erroll.*

Lord Phillips of Sudbury: *I am thoroughly schooled, my Lords, and deeply grateful to – I scarcely dare address him now – the noble Earl Ferrers.*

Earl Ferrers: *The noble Lord!*

Lord Phillips of Sudbury: *Oh my gosh. I shall go back to school...*

[Shortly thereafter...]

Lord Hunt of Kings Heath: *My Lords, it is a great pleasure to welcome the noble Lord, Earl Ferrers, to our debates on –*

Noble Lords: *No!*

Earl Ferrers: *It is the noble Earl, Lord Ferrers. For goodness' sake, the noble Lord is still on the Front Bench. He really ought to get to know the rules and procedures of the House.*

Noble Lords: *Hear, hear!*

The Earl of Erroll: *If noble Lords will indulge me for two seconds, the only person who is the exception here is the noble Duke, the Duke of Montrose. Otherwise, we are all Lords and Ladies. We are Peers, so socially we refer to each other as Lord and Lady. Even a Baroness is a Lady, and we put the true title in front.*

Lord Hunt of Kings Heath: *With the greatest of respect to the noble Lord, the Earl Ferrers –*

Noble Lords: *No!*

Earl Ferrers: *The noble Lord, Lord Hunt, is a very bright noble Lord, and he normally picks up things straight away, but he has made the mistake twice. If he wishes to refer to me as he should, he ought, with respect, to say 'the noble Earl, Lord Ferrers' and not 'the noble Lord, Earl Ferrers'.*

Lord Skelmersdale: *My Lords, while we are in a correcting mood, may I remind the House that we are actually on Report and not in Committee, as amusing as the exchanges have been heretofore?*

House of Lords, 17 November 2010

Lord Gilbert (formerly Dr John Gilbert, Labour MP for Dudley and then Dudley East 1970–97 and a Minister 1974–79) was the scourge of Margaret Thatcher's government during the Defence Committee's inquiry into the Westland Affair in 1986. He also had the rare distinction of going out of government in one office (Minister of State for Defence Procurement) in 1979 and coming back into the same office eighteen years later, in 1997.

More recently he challenged the Lords Hansard writers with his extreme dislike of the Ministry of Defence's love for the A400M transport aircraft:

I regard the decision on the A400M as the most bone-stupid in the forty years that I have been at one end or the other of this building. It is an absolutely idiotic decision. We have a military airlift fleet of C-17s and C-130s. We have total

*interoperability with the United States ... six or seven coun-
tries altogether will be flying the A400M. Flying the C-130,
which it is intended to replace, are 60 countries, with 2,600
C-130Js currently being used. That is the interoperability
that we are losing...*

*Why on earth are we doing this? I once described this
rather vulgarly as a Euro-wanking make-work project and
I do not resile from that. I hope that this time Hansard will
leave that in and not take it out. It was in the next day's
version but Hansard funked it and took it out of the bound
volume. I hope that this is all on the record.*

House of Lords, 12 November 2010

WARREN HASTINGS IN HIS OWN DEFENCE

Warren Hastings, the first Governor-General of Bengal
and of India, 1773–85, was an outstanding administrator
who laid the foundations of the government of British
India over the next 150 years. Far from his later portrayal
as a rapacious plunderer, he was far ahead of his day as
a thoughtful and tolerant administrator, and thought it
vital that Indian social and religious customs should be
understood and respected. In 1784 he said:

*Every application of knowledge and especially such as is
obtained in communication with people, over whom we exercise dominion, founded on the right of conquest, is useful to
the state... It attracts and conciliates distant affections, it
lessens the weight of the chain by which the native peoples*

are held in subjection, and it imprints on the hearts of our countrymen the sense of obligation and benevolence... Every instance which brings their real character will impress us with more generous sense of feeling for their natural rights, and teach us to estimate them by the measure of our own. But such instances can be gained only in their writings; and these will survive when British domination in India shall have long ceased to exist, and when the sources which once yielded of wealth and power are lost to remembrance.

On returning to England, he was impeached by the House of Commons on seven charges of abusing his position, with Edmund Burke, Charles James Fox and Richard Sheridan principally conducting the prosecution before the House of Lords sitting as a court.[*] The case lasted for six years and Hastings was acquitted on all the charges.

Here are the final words from his speech in his own defence:

One word more, my Lords, and I have done. It has been the fashion in the course of this trial, sometimes to represent the natives of India as the most virtuous, and, sometimes, as the most profligate of mankind. I attest their virtue, and offer this unanswerable proof of it. When I was arraigned before your Lordships in the name of the Commons of Great Britain, for sacrificing their honour by acts of injustice,

---

[*] See *Order! Order!* (2009) pp. 139–41.

oppression, cruelty and rapacity, committed upon the princes, nobles and commonalty, of Hindustan, the natives of India, of all ranks, came forward unsolicited to clear my reputation from the obloquy with which it was loaded. They manifested a generosity for which we have no example in the European world. Their conduct was the effect of their sense of gratitude for the benefits they had received during my administration. My Lords, I wish I had received the same justice from my country!

The Trial of Warren Hastings in Westminster Hall

POLITICAL HOSTESSES

In the period 1815–35 it was said that there were seven London hostesses who could get a Commons debate rescheduled if it clashed with one of their dinner parties: Lady Cowper, Lady Jersey, Lady Tankerville, Lady Sefton, Lady Willoughby, Princess Lieven and Princess Esterházy. (Palmerston was said to have had affairs with at least three of them.)

The history of all former attempts at coming to close quarters with the House of Lords Question shows a record of disorder, dissipation of energy, of words and solemn exhortation, of individual rhetoric ... without any definite scheme of action.

A note to Asquith as Prime Minister from Edwin Montagu, his Parliamentary Private Secretary, 1909

I was not going to advertise the existence of the mouse helpline, although it was advertised some time ago. Indeed, I invited Members of the House to telephone when they saw mice. The trouble is that when the person at the other end of the helpline goes to check this out, very often the mouse has gone elsewhere.

The Lord Chairman of Committees (Lord Brabazon of Tara) answering a question in the House of Lords on the control of pests in the Palace of Westminster, 3 March 2010

Sir,

Most of those who are debating the future of the House of Lords appear to have forgotten one of the golden rules of constitutional reform: if the answer is either (a) more politicians or (b) more civil servants, it's the wrong question.

Letter to *The Times*, April 2012.

HOW MANY PEERS?

In June 2012 the House of Lords contained:

- 2 Archbishops
- 24 Bishops
- 23 Law Lords
- 674 Life Peers
- 92 Peers 'under the House of Lords Act 1999' (the former hereditaries)
- **Total 815**
- 30 Peers had leave of absence
- 1 Peer was disqualified by being an MEP
- 12 Peers were disqualified as senior members of the judiciary

Tony Blair's plans for reform of the House of Lords involved the removal of the hereditary peers. As shadow Leader of the Lords, Viscount Cranborne[*], great-great grandson of Prime Minister Salisbury, negotiated a deal with the government whereby 92 hereditary peers would be retained. Unfortunately he omitted to clear this with William Hague, his party leader, admitting graciously that he had *rushed in, like an ill-trained spaniel*.

Hague sacked him. Shortly afterwards he was asked in an interview what effect he thought this would have on his career.

'Career?' asked Cranborne; *'What do you mean, career? I'm not a bank clerk.'*

---

[*] Sitting in the Lords as Baron Cecil of Essendon; now Marquess of Salisbury.

THE HOUSE OF COMMONS

*[Sir Richard Ford MP] did make me understand how
the House of Commons is not to be understood, it being
impossible to know beforehand the success of any small
plain thing.*
Samuel Pepys, *Diary*, 19 December 1666

PRAYERS FOR THE PARLIAMENT
The first detailed reference to prayers being said at the
start of a sitting of the House of Commons occurs in
the first year of the reign of Elizabeth I. The Journal of the
House for 11 February 1558 records:

*This morning Litany was said by the Clerk kneeling and
answered by the whole House on their knees with divers
prayers.*

For much of the next century the same pattern was followed, with the Clerk of the House saying the Litany and the Speaker following with a prayer of his own. Occasionally an ordained minister helped out: in 1601 the minister was paid £10, taken from the end-of-Session collection for the poor, and from the fines paid by MPs who left the Session early.

The first Chaplain to the House to be described as such was Edward Voyce, in 1660. The office became known as the Speaker's Chaplain in the eighteenth century (perhaps because so many relations of Speakers were appointed). The present holder of the office, and the first woman to be appointed, is the Rev. Rose Hudson-Wilkin.

TIMING

Sir Peter Tapsell, Father of the House in the 2010 Parliament, was assistant to Sir Anthony Eden in the General Election campaign of 1955. Eden told Tapsell of advice that he (as a new MP) had received from Lloyd George. 'When you speak in the House of Commons, don't say anything much for the first five minutes. Let the House *fill up*.'

THREE READINGS

Everyone knows that a Bill has to be read three times in order to pass either the Lords or the Commons. Oddly, though, in the Commons the Standing Orders imply, but say nothing directly about there actually having to be three readings. And indeed, on one occasion, in Session

1554–55, it seems that the Commons gave the Bail Bill no fewer than *six* readings.

UNFETTERED BY CONSIDERATIONS OF TASTE

Terry Dicks, Conservative MP for Hayes and Harlington 1983–97, fell into Tom Lehrer's category of *'having a Muse unfettered by considerations of taste'*. Dicks attacked subsidies for the *'fat cats'* who liked opera, which he thought consisted of *'overweight Italians singing in their own language'*, just as ballet was *'men prancing about in ladies' tights'*. He castigated West Indians as *'in general, bone idle ... time they were given a kick in the pants'*. Illegal immigrants were liars, cheats and queue-jumpers who should be sent packing. He advocated the birch for Scottish football hooligans, who he described as *'those pigs from Scotland'*.

The Labour MP Tony Banks said of him: *'His speeches are made additionally entertaining by the looks of horror on the faces of so many of his colleagues on the Conservative benches.'*

Banks also said that Dicks was *'living proof that a pig's bladder on a stick can get elected to Parliament'*.

PARTY DISCIPLINE

Peter Mandelson exercised an iron grip on candidates and policy during the 1997 General Election campaign. Shortly after Labour's victory, a new Labour MP is said to have gone down to the barber's in the House of Commons for a haircut. As the barber combed the rather bouffant hair, he was surprised to find an earpiece. *'I'm sorry, Sir,'* he said. *'I can't cut your hair with that in. Would you mind taking it out?'* *'Not at all,'* said the MP, and did so. Half a minute later he fell forward into the basin in a faint. Somewhat perplexed, the barber gingerly picked up the earpiece and listened. He heard the voice of Peter Mandelson saying, *'Breathe **in**. Breathe **out**. Breathe **in**...'*

SECOND THOUGHTS

The House was moved, That the entry in the Votes of the House, in the 31st of January last, 'That the thanks of the House be given to the Rev. Doctor Nowell for the sermon preached by him yesterday might be read.'
And the same being read accordingly
* Resolved, that the said entry be expunged from the Votes of this House.*
Journal of the House of Commons, 25 February 1772. (Thomas Nowell, then Principal of St Mary Hall, Oxford, and Regius Professor of Modern History, had said some disobliging things about Charles I in the sermon. The House's reaction time appears to have been a little slow.)

I really am serious in thinking – and I have given as pain-ful consideration to the subject as man with children to live and suffer after him can honestly give to it – that representative government is become altogether a failure with us, that English gentilities and subserviences render the people unfit for it, and that the whole thing has broken down since that great seventeenth-century time, and has no hope in it.

Charles Dickens, in a letter to a friend, 30 September 1855

The English are a naturally silent race. The most popular type of hero is the 'strong silent man'. And most of the members of the House of Commons are, at any rate, silent members. Mercifully silent. Seeing the level attained by such members as have an impulse to speak, I shudder to conceive an oration by one of those unimpelled ones... Perhaps I am too nervous. Surely I am too nervous. Surely the House of Commons manner cannot be a natural growth. Such perfect virtuosity in dufferdom can be acquired only by constant practice.

Max Beerbohm, in *Yet Again* (1909)

Dear Sir,

Lord Randolph Churchill desires me to say, in reply to your letter of the 21st inst., that his height is just under 5ft 10in.

I am, Yours faithfully,

Cecil Drummond-Wolff, Secretary

[To two Yorkshiremen who had written to Randolph Churchill after having an argument about his height.]

> *All great things are simple, and many can be expressed in*
> *single words: freedom, justice, honour, duty, mercy, hope.*
> Winston Churchill

The Clerk of the House of Commons has, on assuming office, to make a declaration before the Lord Chancellor which even to the original Elizabethan readers must have appeared pretty confusing. There is no punctuation.

> *I ... do declare that I will be true and faithful and troth I will*
> *bear to Our Sovereign Lady The Queen and to Her Heirs and*
> *Successors I will nothing know that shall be prejudicial to*
> *Her Highness Her Crown Estate and Dignity Royal but that*
> *I will resist it to my power and with all speed I will advertise*
> *Her Grace thereof, or at least some of her Council in such wise*
> *that the same may come to Her Knowledge I will also well*
> *and truly serve Her Highness in the Office of Under Clerk of*
> *Her Parliaments to attend upon the Commons of this Realm*
> *making true entries Remembrances and Journals of the things*
> *done and passed in the same I will keep secret all such matters*
> *as shall be treated in Her said Parliaments and not disclose*
> *the same before they shall be published but to such as it ought*
> *to be disclosed unto and generally I will well and truly do and*
> *execute all things belonging to me to be done appertaining to*
> *the said Office of Under Clerk of the Parliaments.*

The Clerk of the House of Commons is still described in the most formal documents as 'the Under-Clerk of the

Parliaments, to wait upon the Commons'. The Clerk of the Parliaments is his opposite number, the Clerk of the House of Lords, and 'Parliaments' in the plural dates from the times when there were Parliaments only from time to time, so he was, as it were, 'the Clerk of whatever Parliaments there might happen to be'.

> *I hope I never have to face an audience like that.*
> Mike Yarwood, political impersonator, on hearing the first broadcasts from the Commons

The Stamp Act 1765 taxed the American colonists directly for the first time, in order to raise revenue to pay for the British troops stationed in America. The reaction of the colonists was a significant step towards the American Revolution.

THE HOUSE'S SEVEN HOUR SERMON

Tuesday, 17 November 1640 ... '*was the fast day which was kept piously and devoutly; Doctor Burgess and Master Marshall preached before the House of Commons at least 7 houres betwixt them on Jeremiah 50.5 and 2 Chronicles 2.3.*'

The text from Jeremiah Chapter 50 verse 5 was: '*They shall inquire concerning Sion with their faces thitherwards, saying, Come ye, and join yourselves to the Lord in an everlasting covenant that shall not be forgotten.*'

And the text from the Second Book of Chronicles, Chapter 2, verse 3, was: '*And Solomon sent to Hiram the King of Tyre, saying, As thou didst deal with David my father, and didst send him cedars to build an house to dwell therein, even so deal with me.*'

Lots of material there, evidently.

Sir, it is very easy to complain of party Government, and there may be persons capable of forming an opinion of this subject who may entertain a deep objection to that Government... But there are others who shrug their shoulders, and talk in slipshod style upon this head who, perhaps, are not exactly aware of what the objections lead to. These persons should understand that, if they object to party Government, they do, in fact, object to nothing more or less than Parliamentary government. A popular Assembly without Parties – 500 isolated individuals – cannot stand for

five years against a Minister with an organized Government
without becoming a servile Senate.

Benjamin Disraeli, House of Commons, 11 April 1845

MUSCULAR CHRISTIANITY

In the very first Oxford and Cambridge Boat Race in 1829 there was a future Speaker's Chaplain in each boat: Thomas Garnier (Chaplain 1849–57), Worcester, in the Oxford boat; and Charles Merivale (1863–69), St John's, in the Cambridge boat.

Thomas de Quincey said his wife...

...sometimes read to me chapters from more recent works, or parts of parliamentary debates. I saw that generally these were the very dregs and rinsings of the human intellect; and that any man of sound head, and practised in wielding logic with scholastic acuteness, might take up the whole academy of modern economists, and throttle them between heaven and earth with his finger and thumb, or bray their fungus heads to powder with a lady's fan.

From *Confessions of an English Opium Eater*

In the first Session of the 2010 parliament: that is, May 2010 to May 2012, there were 239 separate rebellions by coalition MPs. That was more in two years than the number of rebellions by MPs on the government side in all but three entire parliaments since 1945.

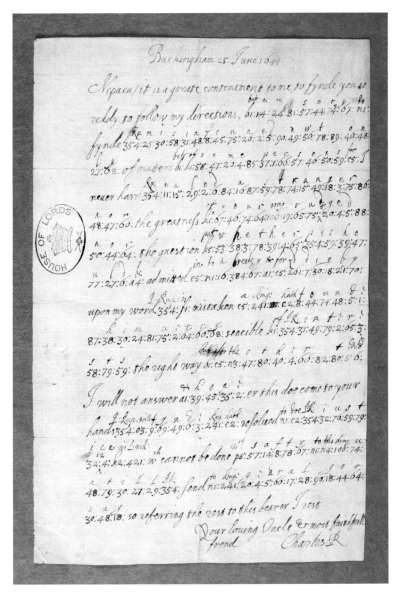

'The Naseby letter' is one of the cache of secret letters of Charles I found on the battlefield of Naseby. Mainly in cipher, it is from the King to Prince Maurice, brother of Prince Rupert. Writing from Buckingham, the King says, '*It's a great contentment to me, to find you so ready to follow my directions*', but he says that Prince Rupert is misinformed '*not only of matters but of some persons*'. © Palace of Westminster

Jeremiah Dyson (1722–76) by Sir Joshua Reynolds. Dyson was Clerk of the House of Commons from 1741 to 1762. He bought the Clerkship for £6,000, or about £750,000 in today's money, but in a remarkable display of public spirit, ended the practice of purchase when he left the Clerkship.

Warren Hastings (1732–1818), first Governor-General of Bengal and of India, 1773–85, by Lemuel Abbot. © Palace of Westminster

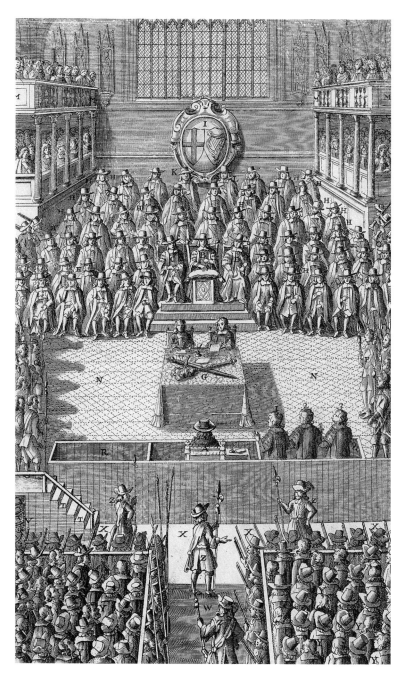

The Trial of Charles I in Westminster Hall, 1649. © Palace of Westminster

"YOU ARE REQUESTED NOT TO SPEAK TO THE MAN AT THE WHEEL."

You are requested not to speak to the man at the wheel by John Leech, *Punch*, 1854. Lord Aberdeen was a frequent butt for cartoonists on account of his relaxed handling of the Crimean War. Like Eden, he had been a very good Foreign Secretary under a strong Prime Minister (in his case Peel), but was less good at the top job. © Palace of Westminster

Mr Fox asleep on the Opposition Benches, drawing by Robert Heron, c. 1800.
© Palace of Westminster

The Cloisters, looking towards St Stephen's Chapel (the Chamber of the House of Commons) five days after the fire of 16 October 1834, by Robert William Billings. © Palace of Westminster

The Rt Rev. David Sheppard, Baron Sheppard of Liverpool (1929–2005), the only ordained minister to have played Test cricket. © Ian Nuttall. Reproduced by kind permission of *The House* magazine.

A curious, sardonic, reticent creature, but able.

Sir Courtenay Ilbert, Clerk of the House of Commons 1902–21, about his successor but two, Sir Gilbert Campion, later Lord Campion.

THE FATHER OF THE HOUSE...

...(there hasn't yet been a Mother of the House, and none is likely soon) is the Member of the House of Commons with the longest continuous service. (Oddly, the senior member of a select committee is calculated by his or her *total* service, whether continuous or not.)

When long-serving Members came into the House at the same General Election, their relative seniority is determined by who took the oath or made affirmation first. It is sometimes said that new Members in safe seats, with an eye on the possibility of being Father of the House forty years later, try to take the oath especially early in the swearing days of a new Parliament.

It is the task of the Father of the House to preside (sitting at the Table rather than in the Speaker's Chair) over the election of the Speaker at the start of a Parliament, or when the office falls vacant.

The present Father of the House is Sir Peter Tapsell, whose unbroken service dates from 1966, although he was also an MP from 1959 to 1964.

His ten most recent predecessors as Father of the House are:

- 2005–10: Alan Williams
- 2001–05: Tam Dalyell
- 1992–2001: Sir Edward Heath
- 1987–92: Sir Bernard Braine
- 1983–87: Sir James Callaghan
- 1979–83: John Parker
- 1974–79: George Strauss
- 1965–74: Sir Robin Turton
- 1964–65: R. A. Butler
- 1959–64: Sir Winston Churchill

AT THE 2010 GENERAL ELECTION...

...the largest constituency in terms of electors was the Isle of Wight, with 109,966 voters.

The smallest constituency in terms of electors was Na h'Eileanan an Iar (formerly Western Isles), with 22,266 voters.

EXTEMPORE

Not only today, but down the centuries, there has been a great variety among MPs of the *ability to speak without notes*. The ability to engage in debate, rather than read some laboured contribution into the record, has always been the mark of the real parliamentarian. This is especially important in the House of Commons, where the tradition of 'giving way' during one's speech, to allow other Members to challenge or question what is being said, has always made for better debate (and is unusual in the world's parliaments). Those who can speak without notes – or with minimal cue-cards – have a huge advantage over those who cannot.

In 1907 Herbert Asquith spoke with power and eloquence for an hour and a quarter on the Licensing Bill. Hansard sent a message asking for his notes, the better to transcribe the speech. Back came a single sheet of paper with the words '*Not so many pubs.*'

DIVISION OF LABOUR

Tam Dalyell served in the House of Commons for forty-three years, first for West Lothian (and so posing the 'West Lothian Question', although it was given its name by Enoch Powell) and then for Linlithgow. He was Father of the House for four years before retiring in 2005. Shortly after his election he became involved in a local issue, to the annoyance of the councillor for that ward. He received a crisp rebuke: '*Westminster, your business. Dog shit, mine.*'

Perhaps unguessably, Tam Dalyell is a sixth cousin of Harry S. Truman.

Select committees: little gatherings of the unwilling, picked from the unfit to do the unnecessary.
'Anonymous' but quoted by Sir Barnett Cocks, Clerk of the House from 1962 to 1973. Given his remark about a select committee being a cul-de-sac down which ideas are lured and then quietly strangled, quite likely to be his own.

Sir Robert Peel is credited with the development of the Tamworth pig, a red-orange, very hardy variety: an excellent bacon pig now rare in the UK. From 1812 at his Drayton Manor estate at Tamworth in Staffordshire, Peel interbred local Tamworths with the 'Irish Grazers' Peel had seen in Ireland in 1809.

Peel was chosen by the Prime Minister to second the Reply to the King's Speech at the start of the 1810 Session, and made a sensational maiden speech, described by the Speaker, Charles Abbott, as '*the best first speech since that of William Pitt*'.

Sir, you have a right to speak, but the House has a right to judge whether they will hear you.

Spencer Compton, when Speaker of the House of Commons 1715–27. He was later 1st Earl of Wilmington, Prime Minister 1742–43

OF CHURCHILL

Without him England was lost for a certainty; with him England has been on the verge of disaster time and again.

Field-Marshal Lord Alanbrooke, Chief of the Imperial General Staff, 1941–46

OF CROMWELL

I will quote certain other words. I do it with great reluctance, because I am speaking of those who are old friends and colleagues of mine, but they are words which, I think, are applicable to the present situation. This is what Cromwell said to the Long Parliament when he thought it was no longer fit to conduct the affairs of the nation: 'You have sat too long here for any good you have been doing. Depart, I say, and have done with you. In the name of God, go.'

Leo Amery (1873–1955), in the House of Commons, 7 May 1940

Speak for England, Arthur!

Leo Amery (1873–1955), to a somewhat flustered Arthur Greenwood, deputising for Clement Attlee, the Leader of the Opposition, who was about to reply to Neville Chamberlain's ambivalence as to whether Britain would come to the aid of Poland.

House of Commons, 2 September 1939.

THE ACADEMIC VIEW

As Sir William Anson, a distinguished writer on the constitution, elected to the House of Commons in 1899, was advancing up the floor of the House to the Clerk of the House to be sworn, there was a conversation between Speaker Lowther and a Member standing beside the Speaker's Chair:

'This is Anson, the great expert on the House of Commons, isn't it?'

'The very man.'

'Well, he will find it very different from what he expected.'

Two Members were sitting in the Smoking Room (in the days before the Health Act 2006, really a Smoking Room). One appears deeply depressed.

'What's the matter, old man?' asks his cheery colleague, hoping to buck him up.

'I've got to go to the constituency tomorrow,' says the sufferer.

'Well, that's not too bad, is it?' says the cheery one. *'I mean, it won't last for that long.'*

'You don't understand,' says the sufferer. *'I'll have to go there **next year as well**.'*

Robert Lowe, a contemporary Liberal MP, said of John Stuart Mill, the giant of nineteenth-century social and political philosophy, who was an MP for Westminster 1865–68: *'He is a little too clever for us in the House. He reasons with a degree of closeness and refinement that some of us, at least, are not quite accustomed to.'*

Mill was hardly diplomatic towards his fellow Members, complaining about *'the tiresome labour of chipping off little bits of one's thoughts, of a size to be swallowed by a set of diminutive practical politicians incapable of digesting them.'*

A WARNING TO ANYONE CHAIRING A POLITICAL MEETING (OR INDEED ANYTHING)

George Bernard Shaw was the principal speaker at a packed meeting. The occupant of the chair began to introduce him ... and went on. And on. And on. There was the occasional false dawn (at least three 'finally's) but after thirty minutes there was no sign of an end. At last it came: *'I now have the singular pleasure, indeed I think I count myself safe in saying the greatest pleasure, in inviting Mr George Bernard Shaw to give us his address.'*

'10, Bloomsbury Terrace,' said Shaw, and stormed out.

THE WHIPS

'Vote early, vote often' – Traditional
'One is enough' – Whips' proverb

> *If you have any doubt, don't go in and listen to the debate; just stay out and vote.*
>
> Jack Weatherill, later Speaker of the House of Commons 1983–92, when Conservative Deputy Chief Whip

DIVISIONS

Edmund Burke was probably the first to argue that the names of Members voting in a Division in the House of Commons should be published, so that their constituents, and the public at large, could call them to account.

In 1810 the diarist Thomas Creevey wrote:

A damned canting fellow in the House, Mr Manning, complained of Members' names being printed as a breach of privilege, and so it would have passed off if I had not showed them that, so far from it being a breach of privilege, it was a vote in King William's time, 'that Members' names should be printed that the country might know who did, and who did not, their duty'.

The Tellers reading out the result of a Division,
Illustrated London News, 18 February 1882

But it was not until 1836 that the names of Members voting on each side were routinely recorded and published with the official record of proceedings, the same year the House changed its method of taking a vote. Up until then, those who wished to vote 'Aye' went out of the Chamber. The Noes sat where they were, and were counted; the Ayes were counted as they came back into the Chamber. After

1836 – not without a lot of opposition from the traditionalists – Members left the Chamber to be recorded as Ayes and Noes in separate Division Lobbies, the system that continues to this day.

BALDNESS

Maurice Orbach (1902–79), Labour MP for Willesden East from 1945, and later for Stockport South, was bald. Unlike many bald men, this troubled him. During the summer recess of 1975 he acquired a toupée. This was an error: the toupée didn't fit and didn't match what hair he had left. His colleagues were decently silent about this until the first big Division after the recess. Orbach was on his way through the Division Lobby, and reached the clerks' desks, where he encountered not only a large crowd of his colleagues, but also the senior Labour Whip, Joe Harper. '*Ee, is tha name Orbach?*' asked Harper. '*I used to know your Dad.*'

TYPO

The government Whips aren't always keen on MPs from their side speaking in legislative committees on the grounds that silence assists securing the legislation. Steve Norris (MP for Oxford East 1983–87 and then for Epping Forest 1988–97) made a memorable intervention in a Standing Committee on the Education (Student Loans) Bill in 1990; nothing to do with the amendment before the Committee at the time, but the Chair was evidently keen to hear the story.

A friend of mine has two sons at Winchester, and the other day the Bursar wrote to him to say that the boarding fees were going up by an extra £2,000 per anum. My friend wrote back to say that it was jolly decent of the Bursar to let him know of this new opportunity, but he would really rather go on paying through the nose, as before.

CHARLES DICKENS...

...whose bicentenary was celebrated in 2012, was in his struggling early days a parliamentary reporter. He said of his experiences:

I have worn my knees by writing on them in the back row of the old Press Gallery. I have worn my feet standing to write in the preposterous pen in the old House of Lords where we used to huddle together like so many sheep, kept in waiting until the Woolsack might want restuffing.

By fierce application Dickens had taught himself Gurney's system of shorthand, and by 1828 he was established as a reporter on *The Mirror of Parliament*, a forerunner of Hansard which produced remarkably full reports of parliamentary debates. Dickens's time as a reporter was a stormy one in Parliament. In March 1831 the first Great Reform Bill was read a second time in the Commons by 302 votes to 301, there was then a dissolution and a General Election notable for its violence, the second

Reform Bill was lost in the Lords, and only in March 1832 did the third such Bill finally pass.

Dickens seems not to have been an admirer of Parliament. In *Sketches by Boz* he says that *'this paper was written before the practice of exhibiting Members of Parliament, like other curiosities, for the small charge of half-a-crown, was abolished'*. Dickens described the House of Lords as *'a conglomeration of noise and confusion'*.

Mr Twemlow's remark in *Our Mutual Friend* that *'the House of Commons is the best club in London'* is often quoted approvingly, but it is more likely to be satirical: that, at a time of widespread social injustice against which Dickens crusaded, the House of Commons was just that: a very good club. He describes Bellamy's refreshment room:

...where divers honourable members prove their perfect independence by remaining during the whole of a heavy debate, solacing themselves with the creature comforts; and whence they are summoned by whippers-in, when the House is on the point of dividing; either to give the 'conscientious votes' on questions of which they are conscientiously innocent of knowing anything whatever, or to find a vent for the playful exuberance of their wine-inspired fancies, in boisterous shouts of 'Divide!', occasionally varied with a little howling, barking, crowing, or other ebullitions of senatorial pleasantry.

A Division Lobby in the House of Commons, 1883

'A Parliamentary Sketch' in *Sketches by Boz* is hardly complimentary, but it shows that Dickens knew his House of Commons:

You see this ferocious-looking gentleman, with a complexion almost as sallow as his linen, and whose large black moustache would give him the appearance of a figure in a hairdresser's window, if his countenance possessed the thought which is communicated to those waxen caricatures of the human face divine. He is a militia officer, and the most amusing person in the House. Can anything be more exquisitely absurd than the burlesque grandeur of his air, as he strides up to the lobby, his eyes rolling like those of a Turk's head in a cheap Dutch clock? He never appears without that

118

bundle of dirty papers which he carries under his left arm, and which are generally supposed to be the miscellaneous estimates for 1804, or some equally important documents. He is very punctual in his attendance at the House, and his self-satisfied 'He-ar, He-ar' is not unfrequently the signal for a general titter.

Dickens's 'county Member' is a recognisable figure in any age:

He can tell you long stories of Fox, Pitt, Sheridan and Canning, and how much better the House was managed in those times... He has a great contempt for all young Members of Parliament, and thinks it quite impossible that a man can say anything worth hearing, unless he has sat in the House for fifteen years at least, without saying anything at all... He is an excellent authority on points of precedent, and when he grows talkative, after his wine, will tell you how Sir Somebody Something, when he was whipper-in for the Government, brought four men out of their beds to vote in the majority, three of whom died on their way home again; how the House once divided on the Question, That fresh candles be brought in; how the Speaker was once upon a time left in the Chair by accident, at the conclusion of business, and was obliged to sit in the House by himself for three hours, until some Member could be knocked up and brought back again, to move the Adjournment; and a great many other anecdotes of a similar description.

And in Bellamy's refreshment room we find:

> *The small gentleman with the sharp nose ... is a Member of Parliament, an ex-Alderman, and a sort of amateur fireman. He, and the celebrated fireman's dog, were observed to be remarkably active at the conflagration of the two Houses of Parliament – they both ran up and down, and in and out, getting under people's feet, and in everyone's way, fully impressed with the belief that they were doing a great deal of good, and barking tremendously. The dog went quietly back to his kennel with the engine, but the gentleman kept up such an incessant noise for some weeks after the occurrence, that he became a positive nuisance. As there have been no more parliamentary fires, however, and as he has consequently had no more opportunities of writing to the newspapers to relate how, by way of preserving pictures he cut them out of their frames, and performed other great national services, he has gradually relapsed into his old state of calmness.*

SOME HOUSE OF COMMONS STATISTICS

The first Session following the 2010 General Election was the longest for 350 years. The passage of the Fixed Term Parliaments Act meant that instead of the Session running from November to November, it had to be rephased to run from May to May so that the fifth Session ended up with a General Election on 7 May 2015 – the first time that a General Election date has been fixed in this way.

One result of the rephasing was that the first Session of the 2010 parliament ran from May 2010 until May 2012. In that Session:

- There were 295 sitting days, averaging 7 hours and 57 minutes each.
- The average length of the House's working papers for each day was 197 pages.
- On average, 40 Early Day Motions were tabled every week, and 1,242 MPs' names were added to existing Motions.
- There were 42 Government Bills and 226 Private Members' Bills.
- 9,785 amendments to Bills were tabled.
- There were 2,288 meetings of select committees, of which 1,392 were evidence hearings.
- There were 76,378,083 hits on the homepage of the Parliament website www.parliament.uk

In the financial year 2011/12 there were 1,038,642 visitors to the Houses of Parliament.

In the financial year 2011/12 41,549 school students came to the Houses of Parliament on visits organised by Parliament's Education Service.

The Houses of Parliament have fourteen buildings in London SW1: the House of Commons has nine, the House of Lords four. One – the Palace of Westminster – is shared.

SITTING HOURS

At the start of the 2010 parliament the sitting times of the House of Commons were: Mondays and Tuesdays, 2.30 p.m.; Wednesdays, 11.30 a.m.; Thursdays, 10.30 a.m.; Fridays, 9.30 a.m.

Before 1570, the House of Commons met from 8 a.m. to 11 a.m. or noon. From 1571 to the Civil War the normal meeting time was 7 a.m. In 1604 the earliest ever start of business took place *at 6 a.m.*

THE MACE

The Mace of the House of Commons symbolises the authority of the House and, beyond that, of the monarch whose arms it bears. The only 'House of Commons Mace' was the *Bauble Mace*, so called from Cromwell's description when dismissing the Long Parliament on 20 April 1653: '*So! Take away that shining bauble there, and lock up the doors. In the name of God, go.*' The Bauble Mace, made in 1649, had the arms of the Commonwealth rather than of the Sovereign.

Upon the Restoration in 1660 the Commons acquired a new Mace with the arms of Charles II (oddly, the Mace was changed in 1670 and 1693, not coinciding with a new reign).

In 1819 the 1660 Mace was brought back into use, and has been used by the Commons ever since.

William Pitt the Younger entered the House of Commons in January 1781. His maiden speech on 26 February was impromptu; Pitt spoke only because a chorus of Members urged him to do so (no doubt wanting to know how he compared with his father, William Pitt, Earl of Chatham). Pitt acquitted himself so well that after his maiden speech Edmund Burke said: '*He is not a chip off the old block. He is the old block itself.*'

Sixteen months later, on 10 July 1782, Pitt was Chancellor of the Exchequer at the age of twenty-three. Seventeen months after that, on 19 December 1783, he became Prime Minister, and remained in office for 17 years and 85 days.

> *From the instant that Pitt entered the doorway* [of the House] *he advanced up the floor with a quick and firm step, his head erect and thrown back, looking neither to the right nor to the left, not favouring with a nod or a glance any of the individuals seated on either side, among many who possessed £5,000 a year would have been gratified even by so slight a mark of attention. It was not thus that Lord North or Fox treated Parliament.*
> Sir Nathaniel William Wraxall

This reserve and self-control was typical of Pitt. In 1786 he had to have an operation (without anaesthetic, of course) to remove a tumour from his face. The great surgeon John Hunter performed the operation at 10 Downing Street. Pitt refused to have his hands tied, saying that he would not move. He asked Hunter how long it would take, and was told six minutes. As Hunter began, Pitt fixed his gaze on the Horse Guards clock. When the operation was finished, Pitt said simply: '*You have exceeded your time by half a minute.*'

Until the Speakership of Charles Abbott (1802–17) it was the practice for the Speaker-Elect, when presenting himself in the House of Lords for the approval of the Sovereign, to profess his utter unsuitability for the job. A fine example is provided by Sir Christopher Yelverton, Speaker 1597–1601, addressing Queen Elizabeth I:

My estate is nothing correspondent for the maintenance of this dignity; my father, dying, left me a younger brother, and nothing to me but my bare annuity. Then, growing to man's estate, and some small practice of the law, I took a wife, by whom I have had many children, the keeping of us all being a great impoverishing to my estate, and the daily living of us all nothing but my daily industry. Neither from my person nor my nature doth this choice arise; for he that supplieth this place ought to be a man big and comely. Stately and well-spoken, his voice great, his carriage majestical, his nature haughty, and his purse plentiful and heavy; but, contrarily, the stature of my body is small, myself not so well-spoken, my voice low; my carriage lawyer-like and of the common fashion, my nature soft and bashful, my purse thin, light, and never yet plentiful.

Yelverton became a distinguished judge. His parliamentary legacy includes this prayer, which he wrote as Speaker and which is still used on special occasions:

Almighty God, by whom alone Kings reign, and Princes decree justice; and from whom alone cometh all counsel, wisdom and understanding; we thine unworthy servants, here gathered together in thy Name, do most humbly beseech thee to send down thy Heavenly Wisdom from above, to direct and guide us in all our consultations; and grant that, we having thy fear always before our eyes, and laying aside all private interests, prejudices, and partial affections, the result of all our counsels may be to the glory of thy blessed Name, the maintenance of true Religion and Justice, the safety, honour and happiness of the Queen, the publick wealth, peace and tranquillity of the Realm, and the uniting and knitting together of all persons and estates within the same, in true Christian Love and Charity one towards another, through Jesus Christ our Lord and Saviour, Amen.

LOVE AND HATE

You are now exhaling upon the constitution of your country all that long-hoarded venom and all those distempered humours that have for years accumulated in your petty heart and tainted the current of your mortified life.
Disraeli to Lord John Russell

Come on in, the blood's lovely.
Labour MP Austin Mitchell (b. 1934) about a Labour Party Conference

LG [Lloyd George] *was born a cad and never forgot it. Winston was born a gentleman and never remembered it.*
Stanley Baldwin, 1937

In 1902 Francis Broxholm Grey Jenkinson, the Clerk Assistant, might have expected to become the Clerk of the House. But he had a problem with the bottle. Instead Sir Courtenay Peregrine Ilbert, a former Member of the Viceroy of India's Law Council, was appointed. Jenkinson wrote to Ilbert on 8 February 1902:

Sir Courtenay Peregrine Ilbert (1841–1924),
Clerk of the House of Commons 1902–21

I feel that I must write to congratulate you on your appointment, and to assure you that as long as I am at the Table, I shall be most willing to give you any information you may require; and therefore wish to say that, while at the Table I shall of course do all the duties of my office to the best of my ability, I must decline to undertake any responsibility in the future beyond these duties.

I trust that our relations at the Table may be friendly as long as I am there.

They were not.

The natural cloud of his understanding ... made his meaning as unintelligible as his conversation was uninteresting.
The Earl of Chatham about the Duke of Grafton

THOMAS CARLYLE (IN HIS BEST CRANKY FORM) ON GLADSTONE:

Gladstone appears to me one of the contemptiblest men I ever looked on. A poor Ritualist; almost spectral kind of phantasm of a man – nothing in him but forms and ceremonies and outside wrappages; incapable of seeing veritably any fact whatever, but seeing, crediting, and laying to heart the mere clothes of the fact, and fancying that all the rest does not exist. Let him fight his own battle, in the name of Beelzebub the god of Ekron, who seems to be his God. Poor phantasm!

No quotation of Carlyle would be complete without:

How thoughtful of God to arrange for Thomas Carlyle to marry Jane Carlyle, thus making two people unhappy instead of four.
Probably the Rev. Sydney Smith, but also attributed to Samuel Butler and Alfred Tennyson

Charles Mohun, 4th Baron Mohun (1675–1712) was an inveterate duellist who stood trial for murder before he was even old enough to attend the House of Lords. He was pardoned for another murder and was eventually killed in a duel by the Duke of Hamilton.

He uses figures as if they were adjectives.
Treasury view of Lloyd George, when Chancellor of the Exchequer

I clearly foresee the day when this vainglorious and immoral people will have to be put down.
The Prince Consort, speaking of the French, in 1860

You can trust all Englishmen except those who talk French.
Prince Otto von Bismarck

A liberal is a man too broad-minded to take his own side in an argument.
J. K. Galbraith

The right honourable Gentleman is reminiscent of a poker. The only difference is that a poker gives off the occasional signs of warmth.
Benjamin Disraeli on Sir Robert Peel

FIRE!
The 9th Earl of Winchilsea spoke in the House of Lords

'*as if he were shouting on a windy day upon Pendennen Heath*' and would emphasise points in debate by waving a large white handkerchief. Winchilsea, enraged by the Duke of Wellington's support for Roman Catholic emancipation, accused him of '*an insidious design for the infringement of our liberties and the introduction of Popery into every department of the State*'.

Arthur Wellesley, 1st Duke of Wellington,
by John Lucas, 1851–52

Wellington demanded of Winchilsea *'that satisfaction which a gentleman has a right to require, and which a gentleman never refuses to give'*. Wellington, the Prime Minister, asked the one-armed Sir Henry Hardinge, Secretary at War, to be his second, and the duel was fought at Battersea Fields on the morning of Sunday 21 March 1829.

Wellington asked Hardinge to pace out the distances. Hardinge paced twelve, and pointed to where Winchilsea was to stand. *'Dammit,'* said Wellington, *'don't stick him up so near the ditch. If I hit him, he will tumble in.'*

When the two men faced each other, Wellington saw that Winchilsea kept his arm at his side, and so deliberately fired wide. Winchilsea then fired in the air, and his second read out a form of words. *'That won't do,'* said the Duke; *'it is no apology.'* An apology was given, the Duke touched his hat, wished them good morning and rode away.

Surprisingly for such a great soldier, Wellington was a notoriously bad shot. During a shoot Lady Shelley (the pretty Lady Shelley, who had caught Wellington's eye) told one of her daughters to *'stand behind the Duke, for he will protect you'*. In after years the daughter realised that that was the only safe place to stand. On one occasion the Duke winged a dog, then a keeper, and finally an old woman doing her washing. The latter complained, rather loudly. Lady Shelley had no sympathy. *'My good woman, this ought to be the proudest moment of your life. You have had the distinction of being shot by the great Duke of Wellington.'*

Lord Shelburne (later the Marquess of Lansdowne), Prime Minister 1782–83, fought a duel with a Scottish MP, Colonel William Fullerton, who accused Shelburne of treason. They fought in Hyde Park and Shelburne was wounded in the groin. But he wrote to a friend saying '*I don't think Lady Shelburne will be any the worse for it.*'

Pitt the Younger once fought a duel on Putney Heath with another MP, George Tierney; but both fired into the air.

Boys do now cry 'Kiss my Parliament' instead of 'Kiss my arse', so great and general a contempt is the Rump [Parliament] come to among all men, good and bad.
Samuel Pepys, *Diary*, 7 February 1660

Yes, I am a Jew; and when the ancestors of the honourable Gentleman were brutal savages in an unknown island, mine were priests in the Temple of Solomon.
Benjamin Disraeli, in reply to a taunt by Daniel O'Connell, a lifelong enemy

It is the trade of the opponent to attack, it is the trade of the newspaper to be indignant, it is the trade of the minister to defend; and the world looks on believing none of them.
Anthony Trollope, in the *New Zealander*, 1855–56

Taxxa fuq l-income.
From a European document on corporation tax debated

by the House of Commons in May 2011, from whose Annex of terms in all EU languages it may be deduced is the Maltese for corporation tax.

I entirely differ with the Government as to the value of precedents. In this case, as in others, precedents are not mere dusty phrases, which do not substantially affect the question before us. A precedent embalms a principle.
Benjamin Disraeli, House of Commons, 22 February 1848

Good Lord, how did this happen? I never meant it to. What am I going to do?
Sir Frederic Metcalfe, on his appointment as Clerk of the House of Commons in 1948. After his retirement Metcalfe was appointed Speaker of the House of Representatives of Nigeria

I have been this morning with Lady Hester Pitt, and there is little William Pitt, not eight years old, and really the clever-est child I ever saw, and brought up so strictly and proper in his behaviour that, mark my words, that little boy will be a thorn in Charles's side as long as he lives.
Lady Caroline Lennox (Lady Holland), the mother of Charles James Fox, writing in 1766

The noble Lord, in this case as in so many others, first destroys his opponent, and then destroys his own position afterwards. The noble Lord is the Prince Rupert of parliamentary discussion; his charge is resistless, but when he returns from the pursuit he always finds his camp in the possession of the enemy.

Benjamin Disraeli, of Lord Stanley (later Lord Derby)

F. E.

F. E. Smith, 1st Earl of Birkenhead, was never one to underplay a case. When asked by Lever Brothers, the soap magnates, for his opinion on a proposed action for defamation, he worked all night on a pile of papers reputedly four feet thick and, fuelled by a bottle of champagne and a dozen oysters, concluded: *'There is no answer to this action in libel, and the damages must be enormous.'* He was right: the newspapers owned by Lord Northcliffe settled for £50,000, more than four times the previous record for libel damages, and about £5.3 million in today's money.

But when as an MP Smith, a violent opponent of the disestablishment of the Welsh Church, attacked the Welsh Disestablishment Bill as *'a Bill which has shocked the conscience of every Christian community in Europe'*, this hyperbole was too much for G. K. Chesterton:

Are they clinging to their crosses, F. E. Smith,
Where the Breton boat-fleet tosses, Are they, Smith?
Do they fasting, trembling, bleeding, wait the news from this our city,

Groaning 'That's the Second Reading!' Hissing 'There is
*   still Committee!'*
If the voice of Cecil falters, if McKenna's point has pith,
Do they tremble for their altars? Do they, Smith?

Russian peasants round their pope, huddled, Smith,
Hear about it all, I hope. Don't they, Smith?
In the mountain hamlets clothing peaks beyond Caucasian
*   pales,*
Where Establishment means nothing, and they never heard
*   of Wales,*
Do they read it all in Hansard with a crib to read it with –
'Welsh Tithes: Dr Clifford Answered.' Really, Smith?

In the lands where Christians were, F. E. Smith,
In the little lands laid bare, Smith, O Smith,
Where the Turkish bands are busy, and the Tory name is
*   blessed,*
Since they hailed the Cross of Dizzy on the banners from the
*   West!*
Men don't think it half so hard if Islam burns their kith and
*   kin,*
Since a curate lives in Cardiff, saved by Smith.

It would greatly, I must own, soothe me, Smith!
If you left this theme alone, Holy Smith!
For your legal cause or civil, you fight well and get your fee;

For your God or dream or devil you will answer, not to me,
Talk about the pews and steeples, and the Cash that goes
    therewith!
But the souls of Christian peoples? Chuck it, Smith!
'Antichrist, or the Reunion of Christendom: An Ode'

F. E. Smith (1872–1930), 1st Earl of Birkenhead,
by Harrington Mann, 1922

As the newly elected MP for Liverpool, Walton, F. E. Smith made what was generally thought to be one of the finest maiden speeches in living memory, attacking the Liberal government for their arrogance after their landslide victory of 1906. The speech (known as '*I warn the Government*') appeared in full in *The Times* the next day. In the course of it he crossed swords with Lloyd George, who was bested:

> *...it was far easier, if one had a strong stomach, to suggest to simple rustics, as the President of the Board of Trade did, that, if the Tories came into power, they would introduce slavery on the hills of Wales.*
>
> The President of the Board of Trade (Mr Lloyd George, MP for Carnarvon Burghs):
>
> *'I did not say that.'*
>
> Mr F. E. Smith said that:
>
> *'...the right hon. Gentleman would no doubt be extremely anxious to forget it if he could, but, anticipating a temporary lapse of memory, I have in my hand the* Manchester Guardian *of January 16, 1906, which contained a report of this speech. I find the right hon. Gentleman said – what would they say to introducing Chinamen at a shilling a day into the Welsh quarries? Slavery on the hills of Wales! Heaven forgive me for the suggestion! I myself have no means of judging how Heaven would deal with persons who thought it decent to make such suggestions. I can only venture to express a doubt whether any honest politician would ever acquit the right hon. Gentleman of having deliberately given the impression to those he thus addressed that if the Conservative Party were returned they were in danger...'*

Fourteen years later, at the age of forty-seven, Smith as Lord Birkenhead was appointed Lord Chancellor by

Lloyd George, by then head of a coalition government. The *Morning Post* called his appointment '*carrying a joke too far*'.

F. E. Smith is very clever, but sometimes his brains go to his head.
Margot Asquith

He had occasional flashes of silence, that made his conversation perfectly delightful.
The Rev. Sydney Smith on Thomas Babbington Macaulay, poet and essayist, but also Secretary at War 1839–41 and Paymaster General 1846–48

He fills a chair.
Samuel Johnson's dismissive view of Lord North

Men shuddered when he took their arm.
Lloyd George of Sir John Simon

That house, which is the hive of the Kingdome, from whence all her honey comes; that house where Justice herself is conceived in their preparing of Laws.
Description of Parliament by John Donne, much better known as a poet and cleric, but also MP for Brackley 1601–04 and for Taunton in the 'Addled Parliament' of 1614.

MAD JACK

Speakers of the House of Commons never have an easy job. But at least the excesses of such as Mad Jack Fuller belong to an earlier era. Fuller (he preferred 'Honest John' Fuller) was born in 1757 and was elected to Parliament at the age of twenty-three, having come into great wealth with his father's estates in Sussex and in Jamaica.

He was a large man '*whose extravagances*,' said *The Times*, '*especially when he visited the House after dinner, were an opprobrium to it*'. Fuller, a staunch supporter of slavery, would bully other Members, telling them '*not to be afraid of the little fellow with the big wig*' (Speaker Abbot), and would swear freely when he addressed the House.

A contemporary account describes him as having entered the House '*in a state of inebriety, and too audibly mistook the Speaker for an owl in an ivy-bush. He was at once named, and handed over to the Serjeant.*'

He finally went too far. On 27 February 1810, when the House was in Committee, he burst in roaring drunk, kicked over a chair that had been placed for Lord Chatham, and swore at the Chairman and anyone else in range. When the House resumed from Committee he was ordered to be taken into custody, broke away from the Serjeant at Arms, who had to summon reinforcements, and was eventually dragged from the Chamber.

William Wilberforce, who witnessed the incident,

compared him to a mad bull. '*Never surely such a scene in the House of Commons,*' he wrote in his diary.

Fuller was an odd mixture. Dreadful as was his daily behaviour, he was also a philanthropist and patron of the arts and sciences (and builder of follies); he commissioned numerous paintings from J. M. W. Turner; and he was the sponsor and mentor of Michael Faraday. He left the House in 1812. He died in 1834 and is buried under a grand stone pyramid in the churchyard of St Thomas à Becket at Brightling, East Sussex.

For a politician to complain about the press is like a ship's captain complaining about the sea.
Enoch Powell

The British people will never vote for a man who does not wear a hat.
Lord Beaverbrook

LOST IN TRANSLATION

Since 2007 the European Union has had 27 Member States, and 23 official languages (with Croatia about to join). A moment's reflection will reveal that there are of course 506 possible language combinations.

The cost of interpretation and translation for all the EU institutions is now over €1.5 billion. The institutions employ 1,500 linguists; between 800 and 1,000 are on duty for each plenary session of the European Parliament.

But all the interpretative power and skill of these resources cannot cope adequately with English, as this political negotiating vocabulary demonstrates...

WHAT THE BRITISH SAY ... WHAT THE FOREIGNER UNDERSTANDS ... AND WHAT THE BRITISH MEAN

I hear what you say	He accepts my point of view	I disagree and do not wish to discuss it further
With the greatest respect	He respects me	I think you are an idiot
That's not bad	That's not very good	That's very good
That's a brave suggestion	They think I am courageous	You are completely insane
Quite good	Quite good	Strangely disappointing
I would suggest...	It's just a suggestion	Bloody well do it or there will be Hell to pay
Oh, by the way	Not important	What I really want to say
I was a bit disappointed that...	Can't matter much	I am incandescent with fury
Very interesting	Good. They are interested	What arrant nonsense

I'll bear it in mind	Excellent. They will do it	I have forgotten it already
I'm sure it was my fault	Why do they think it was their fault?	Obviously, it's your fault
You must come to dinner	I will get an invitation soon	It's not an invitation. I'm just being polite.
I almost agree	She is nearly in agreement	What a nutter!
I have only a few minor comments	They have spotted some typos	This is no good. It needs a total rewrite
Could we consider some other options?	They have not yet decided	If you think we are going with this you are off your trolley

The English, you know, have their virtues: they are a patient people, and loyal, and allow themselves to be governed by the Scots.

Harold Macmillan

THE TOP JOB

The Prime Minister's office is very simply furnished – just a throne and a prayer mat.
Richard Marsh, of Harold Wilson

Eden is the best Prime Minister we've got.
R. A. Butler (1902–82) who was passed over for (or manoeuvred out of) the premiership twice, when first Macmillan and then Douglas-Home got the job

Wab or Hawold?
Brief inquiry by the Marquess of Salisbury, interviewing each member of the Cabinet as to their preference for Eden's successor

She was like a tigress surrounded by hamsters.
John Biffen, of Margaret Thatcher, 1990

Being Prime Minister is the easiest job in the world. Everyone else has an instrument to play. You just stand there and conduct.

James Callaghan, Prime Minister 1976–79

POLITICAL ECONOMY; OR, LORD JOHN IN PEEL'S CLOTHES.

The Queen (loq.).—"Well! It is not the best fit in the world, but we'll see how he goes on!"

Political Economy, or, Lord John [Russell] in Peel's Clothes; The Queen: 'Well! It's not the best fit in the world, but we'll see how he goes on.'

Print by John Leach, 1846

The office of the Prime Minister is what its holder chooses and is able to make of it.

H. H. Asquith, 1926

DOWNING STREET...

...is named after George Downing, who had been head of intelligence for Cromwell. In 1682 Downing started to build what became a terrace of fifteen houses. No. 10 is actually two houses: an older, larger one at the back and part of Downing's terrace at the front. George II offered it as a gift to Sir Robert Walpole, the first Prime Minister; Walpole turned it down, but later accepted it as a (temporary) perk of the job, and the architect William Kent was employed to turn it into a suitably grand house.

William Pitt, who with nineteen years had the longest tenancy, from 1783 to 1801 and 1804 to 1806, called it a *'vast, awkward house'* and more work took place, including the creation of the Cabinet Room in 1796.

In the 1820s John Soane had another go at it, creating the panelled State Drawing Room. The house might have been pulled down altogether if the 1839 plan to demolish all Downing's buildings had gone ahead; but in the 1860s the buildings opposite No. 10 were demolished to make way for George Gilbert Scott's grand Foreign Office. In 1879 fire destroyed No. 12.

When in 1879 Disraeli moved in, he installed hot running water. Electric light arrived in 1894 in place of gaslight and candles, and was followed by telephones. From 1960 to 1963 a major reconstruction project remodelled Nos. 10 and 11, and recreated No. 12. The Prime Minister, Macmillan, and the whole No. 10 staff moved out to Admiralty House, on Whitehall to the north. When they moved back, Macmillan had less than a month of his premiership to run.

Harold Wilson shared a birthday (11 March) with Rupert Murdoch.

Tony Blair shares a birthday (6 May) with Robespierre, Tsar Nicholas II and Orson Welles.

> *Prime Ministers, nowadays, are too busy to do much harm.*
> E. Hilton Young, MP 1915–35, later Lord Kennet

> *Once I leave, I leave. I am not going to speak to the man on the bridge, and I am not going to spit on the deck.*
> Stanley Baldwin, in his resignation statement to the Cabinet, 28 May 1937

Jim Callaghan became Prime Minister on 15 April 1976, at the age of sixty-four years and nine days. He was the only PM to have held the other three great offices of state: Chancellor of the Exchequer, Foreign Secretary and Home Secretary, but he often claimed that his proudest achievement was the provision of cats' eyes on Britain's roads.

CHEQUERS

Near Aylesbury, Buckinghamshire, it is the Prime Minister's official country residence. The origin of the name is unclear; it could be because the first owner of the estate in the twelfth century, Elias Ostiarius (or de Scaccario), was an usher of the Court of the Exchequer, and had the Court's chequerboard on his coat of arms. There has been a house on the site for 900 years; the present Chequers mainly dates from 1565. In 1715, the then owner of the house married John Russell, a grandson of Oliver Cromwell.

In 1909 the house was bought by Arthur and Ruth Lee (the latter an American heiress), later Lord and Lady Lee of Fareham. They set about removing nineteenth-century Gothic 'improvements', restored the house and added 1,000 acres to the estate. They were childless; and, on the grounds that British Prime Ministers no longer came from great landed families with grand houses and palaces to entertain heads of state and other dignitaries, had the idea of giving Chequers to the nation, with its estate, and the house's outstanding collections of Cromwellian and naval pictures and memorabilia, including Cromwell's death mask and Nelson's watch.

The transfer was made by the Chequers Estate Act 1917. The Schedule to the Act set out Lee's wise and yet nostalgic statement of his purpose:

It is not possible to foresee or foretell from what classes or conditions of life the future wielders of power in this country will be drawn. Some may be as in the past men of wealth and famous descent; some may belong to the world of trade and business; other may spring from the ranks of manual toilers. To none of these in the midst of their strenuous and responsible labours could the spirit and anodyne of Chequers do anything but good. In the city-bred man especially, the periodic contact with the most typical rural life would create and preserve a just sense of proportion between the claims of town and country. To the revolutionary statesman the antiquity and calm tenacity of Chequers and its annals might suggest some saving virtues in the continuity of English history and exercise a check upon too hasty upheavals, whilst even the most reactionary could scarcely be insensible to the spirit of human freedom which permeates the countryside of Hampden, Burke and Milton.

Apart from these more subtle influences, the better the health of our rulers the more sanely will they rule, and the inducement to spend two days a week in the high and pure air of the Chiltern hills and woods will, it is hoped, benefit the nation as well as its chosen leaders. The main features of this scheme are therefore designed not merely to make Chequers available as the official country residence of the Prime Minister of the day, but to tempt him to visit it regularly and to make it possible for him to live there, even though his income should be limited to his salary.

The Lees left Chequers for the last time on 8 January 1921 after a farewell dinner. A stained-glass window in the Long Gallery commemorates their gift:

This house of peace and ancient memories was given to England as a thank-offering for her deliverance in the great war of 1914–18 as a place of rest and recreation for her Prime Ministers for ever.

Chequers, by Marcus May, 2005

James Boswell spent the year 1763 in lodgings in Downing Street (not No. 10), in his *London Journal* accounting them '*a good bargain*'.

One of Margaret Thatcher's later Cabinets had a running joke:

Q. What do we do if the PM gets hit by a bus?
A. Get a new bus.

SIR ALEC DOUGLAS-HOME ON TELEVISION...

I fear that I could not conceal my distaste for the conception that the political leader had also to be an actor on the screen. In 1963 I had an unpromising start when I was being made up for some Prime Ministerial appearance; for my conversation with the young lady who was applying the powder and tan went like this:

'Can you make me look better than I do on television?'

'No.'

'Why not?'

'Because you have a head like a skull.'

'Doesn't everyone have a head like a skull?'

'No.'

Since the start of the twentieth century more than half of all British Prime Ministers have had names beginning with A, B or C.

THINGS THEY NEVER SAID

Arriving back at Heathrow after a conference in sunny Guadeloupe during the 1978–79 Winter of Discontent, Jim Callaghan did not say *'Crisis? What crisis?'* That was the headline in *The Sun*, over a photograph of the returning PM.

COLLECTIVE RESPONSIBILITY

Stop a bit! What did we decide? Is it to lower the price of bread or isn't it? It doesn't matter which, but we must all say the same thing.

Melbourne as Prime Minister, calling down the stairs to the departing Cabinet, March 1841

WORKING THE TEA ROOM

When Edward Heath was Prime Minister his friend and Cabinet colleague Peter Walker told him that it would go down well with the party if Heath spent more time in the Commons Tea Room rather than in the fortress of Downing Street. Shortly after recommending this charm offensive Walker was delighted to see Heath in close conversation with backbenchers in the Tea Room. He was less delighted as he walked past to hear Heath say, *'That was a bloody awful speech you made last night.'*

THE CATS OF NO. 10 DOWNING STREET

The current incumbent is Larry, tabby and white, who arrived from Battersea Dogs and Cats Home on 15 February 2011, attracting predictable media attention, being reported to have had *'a long chat with the Prime Minister'* that morning, and immediately being described as *'rodent czar'*.

Predecessors included Rufus of England, also known as Treasury Bill, who seems to have come into office with Ramsay MacDonald; Wilberforce, who served Heath, Wilson, Callaghan and Thatcher; and Humphrey, a particular favourite of John Major, who arrived uninvited at No. 10.

AN OPERATIC COALITION

The plot of *Iolanthe* is of the usual Gilbertian complexity, but in essence Iolanthe, a fairy, has just been pardoned by the Queen of the Fairies for marrying a mortal, and the Queen undertakes to guard the interests of Iolanthe's son Strephon, an Arcadian shepherd who is half-man and half-fairy and is in love with Phyllis, the ward of the Lord Chancellor, who wishes to marry her himself (as do most of the House of Lords). Now read on.

> STREPHON: *My brain is a fairy brain, but from the waist downwards I'm a gibbering idiot. My upper half is immortal, but my lower half grows older every day, and some day or other must die of old age. What's to become of my upper half when I've buried my lower half I really don't know.*
>
> FAIRIES: *Poor fellow!*
>
> QUEEN: *I see your difficulty, but with a fairy brain you should seek an intellectual sphere of action. Let me see... I've a borough or two at my disposal. Would you like to go into Parliament?*
>
> IOLANTHE: *A fairy Member! That would be delightful!*
>
> STREPHON: *I'm afraid I should do no good there – you see, down to the waist, I'm a Tory of the most determined description, but my legs are a couple of confounded Radicals, and, on a Division, they'd be sure to take me into*

the wrong Lobby. You see, they're two to one, which is a strong working majority.

QUEEN: *Don't let that distress you; you shall be returned as a Liberal-Conservative, and your legs shall be our peculiar care.*

LORD SALISBURY

All his life my grandfather retained his interest in science, and he liked to introduce recent scientific innovations into his home. Hatfield was one of the first places to have an intercommunicating telephone. My grandfather enjoyed testing its efficiency, by reciting nursery rhymes down it. Unsuspecting visitors, sitting as they thought alone, would be alarmed to hear, emerging from a mysterious instrument on a neighbouring table, the spectral voice of the Prime Minister intoning:

'Hey diddle diddle,

The cat and the fiddle...'

My grandfather was also a pioneer in installing electric light. This was even more alarming to the guests than the telephone. The naked, uninsulated wires stretched on the ceiling of the Long Gallery would suddenly burst into flames. My grandfather, conversing below, would look up; he or his sons would nonchalantly toss up a cushion to put the flames out and then resume their conversation.

Lord David Cecil, in *The Cecils of Hatfield House*

LORD SALISBURY ON...

...Eton: *Nothing is taught at Eton which people wish their sons to know.*

...Australia: *No island can be better for the yearly admixture of two thousand select villains to its population.*

...lawyers: *The barrister is at best a tolerated evil. He derives his living from the fact that the law is unintelligible.*

...constituents: *An hotel infested by influential constituents is worse than one infested by bugs. It's a pity you can't carry round a powder insecticide to get rid of vermin of that kind.*

Salisbury, not a musician, said he enjoyed the music of Brahms because it was noisy.

> *Nowhere is there a man who has so much power and so little to show for it.*
> Gladstone on the office of Prime Minister

As Prime Minister (1828–30 and 1834) the Duke of Wellington found the indiscipline of his Cabinet colleagues infuriating:

> *...they agree to what I say in the morning and then in the evening they start up with some crochet which deranges the whole plan. I have not been used to that in the early part of my life. I have been accustomed to carry on things*

in quite a different manner: I assembled my officers and laid down my plan, and it was carried into effect without more words.

CURZON

My name is George Nathaniel Curzon,
I am a most superior person.
My face is pink, my hair is sleek,
I dine at Blenheim twice a week.
From *The Masque of Balliol*, 1875

A hamper is undoubtedly requisite under the present circumstances. It must contain several pots of superior jam.
Lord Curzon, in a letter home from school, aged nine

This omnibus business is not what it is reported to be. I hailed one at the bottom of Whitehall and told the man to take me to Carlton House Terrace. But the fellow flatly refused.
Lord Curzon, connecting with everyday life

Curzon peaked too soon; the rest of his life was a failure by comparison:

In 1898 he was created Viceroy of India, an office filled with pomp and ceremony, at the youthful age of thirty-nine. In his train followed long strings of elephants and retinues of gaily colourful servants. But his years of semi-kingship came to an end in 1905, when at forty-six years he left India an angry and embittered man. For all the rest of his life Curzon was influenced by his sudden journey to heaven at the age of thirty-nine and then by his return seven years later to earth, for the remainder of his mortal existence.

Lord Beaverbrook

Eighteen years after his return from India, when Andrew Bonar Law resigned as Prime Minister in May 1923, Curzon was certain that he would be asked to form an administration. When a telegram from Lord Stamfordham, George V's private secretary, summoned him to London, he thought the thing was in the bag. Driving up from Montacute, the splendid Elizabethan house he rented in Somerset, he laid his plans. *'I shall use No. 10,'* he told his wife, *'only for official purposes. We shall still live and entertain at Carlton House Terrace. I shall remain Curzon, even though Prime Minister.'*

Hubris awaited. After a long wait at Carlton House Terrace, Lord Stamfordham finally arrived, only to tell Curzon that the King had decided to send for Stanley Baldwin. Curzon was devastated, and burst into tears. *'Not even a public figure,'* he said of Baldwin, through his sobs. *'A man of no experience. And of the utmost insignificance.'*

A. J. Balfour was probably the principal agent of Curzon's greatest disappointment; greatly disliking

Curzon, it was he who advised the King to send for Baldwin. Curzon was financially dependent on his rich wife Grace, the second Lady Curzon. On being told that Curzon would be so disappointed not to be PM, Balfour said, '*Oh, I don't know. He may have lost the hope of glory but he still retains the means of Grace.*'

No more than the whiff of scent on a lady's pocket-handkerchief.
Lloyd George's assessment of Balfour's place in history

He has a natural gift for the counterfeit.
Aneurin Bevan, of Stanley Baldwin

I like Mr Baldwin. He promises nothing and keeps his word.
Anonymous

THE OLDEST SERVING PRIME MINISTERS AT RETIREMENT FROM THE OFFICE ARE:

- Gladstone, 84
- Palmerston and Churchill, both 80
- Disraeli, 75
- Russell, 73
- Salisbury, 72
- Portland, Campbell-Bannerman and Chamberlain, all 71
- Wilmington, 70

Neville Chamberlain was the first Prime Minister to fly.

> *Whichever party is in office, the Treasury is in power.*
> Harold Wilson

> *There are three classes which need sanctuary more than others: birds, wild flowers and Prime Ministers.*
> Stanley Baldwin

The last private tenant of 10 Downing Street was a Mr Chicken, who moved out in 1735, and Sir Robert Walpole moved in.

The first mention of the office of Prime Minister in statute is in the Chequers Estate Act 1917.

Attlee was devoted to, but also somewhat in awe of, his determined, articulate wife Violet:

> *Mr Attlee, as he then was, never addressed a word to me, except that, when he first got in the car he would say 'Good morning, George' and when I finally dropped him each evening, he would say 'Good night, George'. Otherwise, not a word. The only time he ever spoke to me was once, when we were driving to Chequers for the weekend, a car overtook us and nearly sent us into the ditch.*
>
> *Mr Attlee said furiously 'Who's that bloody fool?'*
> *I said: 'That was Mrs Attlee, Sir.'*

'Best say no more about it.'
Attlee's official driver when Attlee was Prime Minister

Paul Johnson, interviewing Attlee on television, recalled his disconcerting habit of saying, in answer to a question, *'What's your next question?'*

From 12 May 2010 to 12 June 2012 the Prime Minister's Office replied to 136,000 letters.

Your Secretary of State will wish to consider how to proceed in the light of the Prime Minister's firmly held views.
Note from No. 10 to Norman Fowler's private secretary, March 1986. Fowler was Secretary of State for Health, and had advocated a frank public approach to the dangers of Aids. The Prime Minister (Margaret Thatcher) disagreed.

LIFE AND DEATH

Benjamin Disraeli, on his deathbed, having been told that Queen Victoria wanted to visit him: *What's the use? She would only want me to take a message to Dear Albert.*

SOME LAST WORDS
Sir Thomas More [upon mounting the scaffold]:

I pray you, Mr Lieutenant, see me safe up; and for my coming down, I can shift for myself... I die the King's good servant, but God's first.

Then to the executioner he said:

Thou wilt do me this day a greater benefit than ever any mortal man can be able to give me. Pluck up thy spirit, man, and be not afraid to do thy office. My neck is very short; take heed therefore that thou strike not awry.

As he laid his head on the block, he positioned his beard so that it would not be cut by the axe: *'For that had never committed treason.'*

Sir Thomas More, Speaker in 1523, portrait after Holbein

Putting off his doublet and gowne, he desired the headsman to shew him the Axe, which not being suddenly granted to him, he said 'I prithee, let me see it, dost thou thinke I am afraid of it;' so it being given unto him, he felt along the edge of it and smiling spake unto Mr Sheriffe saying, 'this is a sharp medicine, but it is a medicine that will cure all diseases'.

Sir Walter Raleigh, executed in Old Palace Yard, Westminster, 29 October 1618, described by Sir Thomas Overbury in 1648

CONDEMNED

Whereas Charles Stuart, King of England, is and standeth convicted, attainted and condemned of High Treason and other high crimes; and sentence upon Saturday last was pronounced against him by this court, to be put to death by the severing of his head from his body; of which sentence execution remaineth to be done; These are therefore to will and require you to see the said Sentence executed, in the open street before Whitehall, upon the morrow, being the thirtieth day of this instant January, between the hours of ten in the morning and five in the afternoon, with full effect. And for so doing, this shall be your warrant.

Death Warrant of Charles I, 1649

The Death Warrant of Charles I

Charles I, on the morning of his execution (Tuesday 30 January 1649), to his servant Herbert:

Let me have a shirt on more than ordinary, by reason the season is so sharp as probably may make me shake, which some observers may imagine proceeds from fear. I fear not death. It is not terrible to me. I bless my God I am prepared.

Charles was kept waiting for four hours, from ten until two, before being taken to the scaffold. There, after his last speech, he said to Bishop Juxon: '*I go from a corruptible to an incorruptible crown, where no disturbance can be, no disturbance at all.*' Then he said to the headsman: '*Strike when I put my arms out this way.*' His hair came loose, and the headsman rearranged it. The King, thinking he was going to strike, said '*Stay for the sign*'; and then gave it.

Eleven years later Samuel Pepys described the death of one of the regicides (those who had signed the King's death warrant):

13th October 1660 – I went to Charing Cross, to see Major General Harrison hanged, drawn and quartered; which was done there, he looking as cheereful as any man could do in that condition. He was presently cut down, and his head and heart shown to the people, at which there were great shouts of joy...

Pepys then returned home and spent the afternoon '*setting up shelfes in my studye.*'

Charles II: '*I am sorry, gentlemen, for being such a time a-dying.*'

THE LAST SUNDAY OF CHARLES II

I can never forget all the inexpressible luxury and prophaneness, gaming, and all dissoluteness, and as it were total forgetfulness of God (it being Sunday evening) which this day se'nnight I was witnesse of, the King sitting and toying with his concubines, Portsmouth, Cleaveland, and Mazarine, etc.; a French boy singing love-songs in that glorious gallery, whilst about 20 of the greate courtiers and other dissolute persons were at basset round a large table, a bank of at least £2,000 [about £330,000 in today's money] *in gold before them, upon which two gentlemen who were with me made reflections with astonishment. Six days after, all was in the dust.*
From *The Diary of John Evelyn*, February 1685

Restless he rolls from whore to whore; a merry monarch, scandalous and poor.
John Wilmot, 2nd Earl of Rochester

Wilmot was responsible for the more famous lines:

We have a pretty witty king,
And whose word no man relies on.
He never said a foolish thing,
And never did a wise one.

To which when he heard it Charles said: *'That's true, for my words are my own, but my actions are those of my ministers.'*

Viscount Castlereagh: *'Oh, Bankhead* [his doctor] *I am glad you are there. Let me fall into your arms ... it is all over.'*

Nancy Astor: *'Jakie, is it my birthday or am I dying?'* (Her son replied: *'A bit of both, Mother.'*)

Winston Churchill: *'Oh, I'm so bored with it all.'*

Queen Elizabeth I: *'All my possessions for a moment of time.'*

King George V's last words are supposed to have been *'How is the Empire?'* More plausible from a plain-speaking sailor King was *'Bugger Bognor!'* when comforted by Queen Mary with the thought that he would be able to convalesce there. A few years ago, a literary competition set the task of interpreting from *'How is the Empire?'* what the King-Emperor might actually have said if he had been slightly misheard. The winners were...

The last words of a sporting King: *'Howzat, Umpire?'* and (referring to Mrs Simpson): *'How is that vampire?'*

OVERDONE?

Mansfield was a man of great qualities and accomplishments, but even so...

Sacred

To the immortal memory of

WILLIAM MURRAY, EARL OF MANSFIELD

Late Lord Chief Justice of England

Who during a course of Thirty Years and upwards, not only discharged the duties of that high office with unexampled assiduity, and unquestionable reputation, but happily uniting

The Wisdom of Socrates

The Eloquence of Cicero

The Harmony of Virgil, and

The Wit and pleasantries of Horace

With the beauties of his own unbounded Genius, became and was confessedly the brightest Ornament of human Nature, that any Age or Country has hitherto been able to boast of.

The venerable Peer having passed the age of Fourscore, and finding his corporeal Powers too feeble much longer to display his wonderful Talents with their wonton Energy, withdrew himself from the Bench; and willing to appear with those Talents undiminished at the Throne of his Divine Creator by whom he had been so peculiarly and abundantly endued, shook off the Clog of Mortality in his 89th year

The Noble Lord having shaken off the Clog of Mortality, you might have thought that that was enough, but no...

And as an Eagle, winge'd his airy flight,
Through Death's pale Shade and all-surrounding night,
Up to the happy realms of everlasting Light;
Where, welcomed by the social Powers Divine,
Freely with them drinks celestial Wine;
While, here, Philosophy remains to mourn
Her Fav'rite fled, fled never to return,
Until his God shall at the Judgement Day
With his bright Soul reanimate his Clay,
And all with him to dwell from hence to Heav'n convey.

William Murray, 1st Earl of Mansfield, engraving by
Francesco Bartolozzi after Reynolds, 1786

Evelyn Levett Sutton, Speaker's Chaplain 1827–30, died on 26 January 1835 *'attacked with an apoplexy while reading the ninth commandment* [thou shalt not bear false witness against thy neighbour] *in Westminster Abbey.'*

Also in Westminster Abbey...

Erected by
The *King* and *Parliament*
As a Testimony to
The Virtues and Abilities
of
WILLIAM PITT, EARL OF CHATHAM
During whose Administration,
In the Reigns of *George the Second* and *George the Third*
Divine Providence
Exalted Great Britain
To a Height of Prosperity and Glory
Unknown to any former age
Born 15th Nov., 1708
Died 11th May, 1778

I am ready to meet my Maker. Whether my Maker is prepared for the great ordeal of meeting me is another matter.
Winston Churchill

Memorial to William Pitt, Earl of Chatham,
in Westminster Abbey

In St Margaret's, Westminster (the parish church of the
House of Commons):

In Parliament, a Burgess *Cole* was placed,
In *Westminster* the like for many years,
But now with Saints above his Soul is graced
And lives a Burgess with Heav'n's Royal Peers
Died 1597

SEX...

The pleasure is momentary, the position ridiculous, and the
expense damnable.
Philip Stanhope, 4th Earl of Chesterfield (1694–1773)

*I would heartily wish that you may often be seen to smile,
but never heard to laugh while you live. Frequent and loud
laughter is the characteristic of folly and ill-manners. It is
the manner in which the mob express their silly joy at silly
things and they call it being merry. In my mind there is
nothing so illiberal, and so ill-bred, as audible laughter. I am
neither of a melancholy nor a cynical disposition, and am as
willing and as apt to be pleased as anybody; but I am sure
that since I have had the full use of my reason nobody has
ever heard me laugh.*

Chesterfield, in his *Letters to his Son,* which were
described by Johnson as teaching '*the morals of a whore,
and the manners of a dancing-master*'.

As Lord Stanhope, Chesterfield entered the House of
Commons as Member for St Germans in 1715 and made
his maiden speech on the impeachment of the Duke of
Ormonde. The next speaker in the debate was extrava-
gantly complimentary, but pointed out that as Stanhope
was still under twenty-one he had been improperly
returned and was liable to a fine of £500 for having
spoken. Stanhope is supposed to have bowed low and to
have left immediately for the Continent.

THE TRIAL OF SIR THOMAS MORE

More, briefly Speaker of the House of Commons in 1523,
and from 1529 to 1532 Chancellor of England, was tried
for treason in Westminster Hall on 1 July 1535. He was

convicted on the almost certainly perjured evidence of Richard Rich, the Solicitor General (who himself became Speaker briefly in 1536) that More had in his presence denied that the King was the legitimate head of the Church.

More said in his defence:

Can it therefore seem likely to your Lordships, that I should in so weighty an affair as this, act so unadvisedly, as to trust Mr Rich, a man I had always so mean an Opinion of, in reference to his Truth and Honesty ... that I should impart only to Mr Rich the Secrets of my Conscience in respect to the King's Supremacy, the particular Secrets, and only point about which I have been so long pressed to explain myself? Which I never did, nor ever would reveal, when the Act [of Succession] *was once made either to the King himself, or to any of his Privy Counsellors, as is well known to your honours, who have been sent on no other account at several times by his Majesty to me in the Tower. I refer it to your Judgments, my Lords, whether this can seem credible to any of your Lordships.*

The Court took fifteen minutes to find More guilty, and he was executed five days later.

In the North Aisle of Westminster Abbey:

To the memory of
WILLIAM WILBERFORCE
Born in Hull, Aug. 24, 1759; died in London, July 29, 1833

*For nearly half a century a member of the House of
Commons, and for six parliaments during that period
one of the two representatives of Yorkshire. In an age and
country fertile in great and good men, he was among the
foremost who fixed the character of their time; because,
to high and various talents, to warm benevolence, and
to universal candour, he added the abiding eloquence of
a Christian life. Eminent as he was in every department
of public labour, and a leader in every work of charity,
whether to relieve the temporal or spiritual wants of his
fellow men, his name will ever be specially identified with
those exertions which, by the blessing of God,
removed from England the guilt of the African
Slave Trade
And prepared the way for the
abolition of slavery in every colony
in the Empire. In the prosecution of these objects he
relied not in vain on God: but in the progress he was
called on to endure great obloquy and great opposition.
He outlived, however, all enmity, and in the evening of his
days withdrew from public life and public observation
to the bosom of his family. Yet he died not unnoticed
or forgotten by his country: the Peers and Commons of
England, with the Lord Chancellor and the Speaker at
their head, in solemn procession from their respective
Houses, carried him to his fitting place among the mighty
dead around, here to repose, till through the merits of
Jesus Christ, his only Redeemer and Saviour, whom in his*

life and in his writings he had desired to glorify,
he shall rise in the resurrection of the just.

WHY IS THERE ONLY ONE MONOPOLIES COMMISSION?
Anonymous graffito

A lawyer is a learned gentleman who rescues your estate
from your enemies and keeps it himself.
Henry Brougham, Lord Chancellor 1830–34. Brougham
was instrumental in turning Cannes from a fishing village
into a fashionable resort. He died there in 1868

Well, I thought it was good. It must have been good, for
it contained, so far as I know, all the platitudes known to
the human race, with the possible exception of 'Prepare
to meet thy God' and 'Please adjust your dress before
leaving'.
Winston Churchill on a platitudinous speech about the
League of Nations

I never offered an opinion until I was sixty, and then it was
one which had been in our family for a century.
Benjamin Disraeli

Steadily towards women and drink, Mr President.
F. E. Smith, when asked by President Woodrow Wilson
(whom he greatly disliked) what in his opinion was the
trend of the modern English undergraduate.

*I was never a bird on the unpinioned wing ... when I got up to
speak, I always knew precisely where every noun and adjec-
tive would go and how every piece of punctuation would bed
into my speech. By contrast, the best parliamentary orators,
like Lloyd George, F. E. Smith, Timothy Healy the Irishman,
or even that shit Aneurin Bevan, their phrases were dictated
by some inner God within.*

Winston Churchill

'THE USUAL CHANNELS'

Shorthand for the private conversations that take place
between the business managers for the government and
opposition, determining what parliamentary business
shall be taken when, and for how long. Always confiden-
tial, and extraordinarily effective in ensuring that the
wheels stay oiled. When – as occasionally happens – an
opposition withdraws from 'usual channels' discussions,
both sides usually regret it.

The system has its critics, mainly because of its secrecy.
Tony Benn described the usual channels as *'the most
polluted waterway in Europe'*. If, as expected, a formal
business committee takes a hand in the organisation
of business in the Commons, the relationship with the
usual channels will be crucial.

IMPERCEPTIBLE?

Two thirds of the whole ... is collected, without difficulty or friction, without any necessity for the taxpayer to draw a cheque or even open his purse, and almost without his being made aware that he is being taxed at all – I said, almost.

H. H. Asquith, on deduction of tax from dividends at source, Budget Speech, 1908

PALMIER DAYS

In the latter days of the nineteenth century most House of Commons clerks lived an enviably relaxed and expansive life. Here is a clerk in the early 1890s:

All these labours overtaxed my strength, and in the month of July I was fairly worn out. I was advised by Dr Herman Weber to try the Homburg waters and I was urged to start without delay. But this I could not do in the heat of the Session without urgent necessity, so I waited until within a few days of the Prorogation, when I started for Homburg accompanied by my wife. Having spent the usual month at that gay watering place, water-drinking, promenading, dining and idling, we went to Switzerland and returned via Paris to England early in November, after an absence of nearly three months. My health was certainly improved, if not by the waters, by the rest and recreation I needed so greatly. Our Autumn was spent partly in Town and partly in visits to Lord Eversley at Heckfield, Lord Egerton at Tatton, and other friends in the country.

The present anthologist can admit to spending ten weeks

sailing to the Arctic Circle and back in the summer recess of 1974, but those days now seem as far distant as the 1890s.

DOG-BREEDERS

John Gilbert King, one of two MPs for the Irish seat of King's County 1865–68, is credited with the development of the red setter; and Dudley Coutts Marjoribanks, MP for Berwick-upon-Tweed three times between 1853 and 1881, first bred the golden retriever.

YOUR BUSINESS...

... is not to govern the country, but to call to account those who do.

These words of Gladstone's are often quoted as a neat encapsulation of the role of Parliament compared with that of government. But the context in which he first said them was one of fierce denial that the House of Commons had a role in calling the government to account over its handling of the Crimean War.

How can you inquire into the past of the Sebastopol expedition without examining the present and the future? How is it possible that you can conduct the inquiry with respect to what you may call the past, without – not damaging, but absolutely ruining the present and the future? The real truth is this, that if this Motion be anything ... it is a Motion that the House of Commons cannot pass without violating the laws which fix its place in the constitution, because, if the Motion means anything, it means taking the conduct of the expedition out of the hands of the Government. It seems to me that ... what you mean to imply is, in a legitimate form, your want of confidence in an existing Administration ... but is it really to be supposed that the inquiry now proposed is to be entrusted to a Select Committee?

Speech upon the Motion: *That a Select Committee be appointed to inquire into the condition of our Army before Sebastopol, and into the conduct of those Departments of the Government whose duty it has been to minister to the wants of that Army.* House of Commons, 29 January 1855

THE SPEAKER'S STATE COACH...

... was made for William III, and was later presented to the Speaker of the House of Commons by Queen Anne. Gorgeously painted and gilded, it is probably the oldest such coach in existence. It was last used by Speaker George Thomas to travel to and from St Paul's Cathedral for the wedding of the Prince of Wales and Lady Diana Spencer in 1981. Most people were surprised it got there, and even more surprised it got back, as both axles were bowed and the coach was showing its age in a number of other ways. More recently it has undergone complete restoration and is on display at the Carriage Museum at Arlington Court, near Barnstaple in Devon.

When riding in the State Coach on a State occasion, the

Speaker was entitled to the magnificent escort of ... one Trooper of the Household Cavalry.

> **Madeleine Moon** (Bridgend): *May I reassure the hon. Gentleman – I said this in an earlier intervention – that I, too, was working last night. I was looking at innovation, skills, quality engineering jobs and engineering development in Wales. That was important. The fact that I was not at No. 10 was a matter of complete imbuggerance to me.*
>
> **Mr Deputy Speaker** (Mr Nigel Evans): *Order. What was that word? Is it Welsh?*
>
> **Mrs Moon**: *I apologise. It is a Welsh expression.*
>
> House of Commons, 1 March 2012

DESIDERATA

Also as every one of the Parlement house is free for his owne person, for all manner of sutes to be commenced against him: so also are his Servants free, and not to be troubled nor molested but being troubled, have the like remedie as the Maister hath or may have.

Also no manner of person being not one of the Parlement house: ought to enter or come within the house, as long as the sitting is there: upon pain of imprisonment or suche other punishment, as by the house shall be ordered and adjudged.

Also every person of the Parlement ought to keep secret

and not to disclose the secrets and things spoken and doon in the Parliament house, to any manner of person unless he be one of the same house; on pain to be sequestered out of the house, or otherwise punished, as by the order of the house shall be appointed.

Also none of the Parlement house ought to departe from the Parlement: without speciall leave obteyned of the Speaker of the house, and the same his licence be also recorded.

Also when any Knight, Citizen or Burgess dooth enter and come into the lower house, he must make his dutiful and humble obeysaunce at his entry in: and then take his place. And you shal understand that every such person ought to be grave, wise and expert: so ought he to show himself in his Apparail, for in times past: none of the councellors of ye Parlement came otherwise than in his gown, or girded with weapon, for the Parlement house is a place for wise, grave and good men, to consult, debate and advise how to make Lawes, and orders for the common welth, and not to be armed as men redy to fight, or to trye matters by the Swoord.

From *The Order and Usage of how to keep a Parlement in England in these days*, by John Hooker, MP for Exeter in the Parliament of 1571

A SNOLLYGOSTER...

...is a fellow who wants office, regardless of party, platform

or principles, and, when he wins, gets there by the sheer force of talknophical assumnacy.

Columbus Dispatch, October 1895

OF THE CLERK OF THE LOWER HOUSE

There is only one Clerk belonging to this house, his office is to sit next before the Speaker, at a Table upon which he writeth and layeth his books.

He must make true entrie of the recordes and Billes of the house, as also of all the orders thereof.

The Billes appointed unto him by the Speaker to be red: hee must read openly, plainly and sensibly.

The Billes which are to be engrossed: hee must doo it...

He may not be absent at any time of sitting, without speciall licence.

He ought to have for every private Bil passed and enacted: forty shillings.

He hath allowed unto him for his charges (of the King) for every Session: ten pounds.

From *The Order and Usage of how to keep a Parlement in England in these days*, by John Hooker, MP for Exeter in the Parliament of 1571

The Clerk of the Parliaments (Clerk of the House of Lords) received £3 (£1,200 in today's money) for every private bill passed, against £2 (£800 today) for the Clerk of the Commons. In 1571 the latter (Fulke Onslow) received £24 (£9,600) for private bills, more than twice his £10 (£4,050) stipend.

THE CLERK OF THE CROWN IN CHANCERY...

... is the only commoner to sign his name with his surname only, like a peer, on every document that passes under the Great Seal. This is a survival from the Middle Ages, when clerks signed with their unadorned surname. (Even today, judgments of French and European Union courts are signed by the judges with their surname only.) The office dates at least from 1350, and in 2012 Ursula Brennan, the first woman to be Clerk of the Crown, was appointed. The Clerk of the Crown is an officer of both Houses of Parliament.

The first use of the Great Seal to authenticate a document authorised by the monarch was by Edward the Confessor. Almost every monarch since then has had his or her own design for the Great Seal. The short reign of Edward VIII meant that he never had his own design and continued to use the Seal of his father, George V.

Because the wax used for sealing has a high melting point, the silver used for the Seal itself wears out; Queen Victoria had four Great Seals during her 63-year reign, although that included one to reflect her change of style and title when she became Empress of India on 1 May 1877. The present Queen has had only two in sixty years; one dating from 1953 and a new design in 2001.

Dark green wax is used for letters patent conferring

peerages; blue for documents relating to the Royal Family, and scarlet for appointments and other affairs of state.

There is a Welsh Seal, used to seal, and so bring into force, letters patent signed by the Queen giving Royal Assent to Bills passed by the National Assembly for Wales. The Queen formally delivered this Seal into the custody of the First Minister of Wales at a meeting of the Privy Council at Buckingham Palace on 14 December 2011.

The Great Seal of Scotland (*Seala Mòr na h-Alba* in Gaelic), of which the first known impression dates from 1094, was until 1885 in the custody of the Keeper of the Great Seal of Scotland. After 1885 each Secretary of State for Scotland was also Keeper, until 6 May 1999, when with Scottish devolution the duty passed to the First Minister of Scotland.

The Great Seal of Queen Elizabeth I, here on a Royal Commission for the proroguing of Parliament

The Great Seal of Northern Ireland was created in 1922 'to be used for all matters in Northern Ireland for which the Great Seal of Ireland was theretofore used'.

The Clerk of the Crown is Registrar of the Court of Claims, which determines the rights of those claiming to be entitled to perform ancient services of honour at a Coronation. For this, the Clerk of the Crown is given a bolt of scarlet cloth, from which to make a robe or gown for the Coronation.

The War Office kept three sets of figures: one to mislead the public; another to mislead the Cabinet; and the third to mislead itself.
H. H. Asquith

No amount of education will make women first-rate politicians. Can you see a woman becoming a Prime Minister? I cannot imagine a greater calamity for these islands than to be put under the guidance of a woman in 10 Downing Street.
Margot Asquith, 1943

Generally speaking the Press lives on disaster.
Clement Attlee, 1956

Judgement which is needed to make important decisions on imperfect knowledge in a limited time.
Clement Attlee, on the art of politics

AN HOSPITABLE CORRESPONDENCE

I go tomorrow to Bucklebury, and shall be back on Saturday, on which it would be a great pleasure to meet you in town; but for God's sake to not stay longer than Sunday, because it is most certain our patriots design some gallant thing to open the session with, and that is what, out of kindness to them, everyone should oppose. Though I believe in a little time all the endeavours of their friends to keep 'em on their legs will prove ineffectual. As to whores, dear friend, I am unable to help thee. I have heard of a certain housemaid who is very handsome: if she can be got ready against your arrival, she shall serve for your first meal.

Adieu, ever most entirely, Harry

Henry St John (1678–1751), later Viscount Bolingbroke, an able libertine, and leader of the emerging Tory Party, to Thomas Coke, a fellow MP, in 1704

To succeed in politics, it is often necessary to rise above your principles.

Anonymous

I won't say it's the route to riches but I read almost nothing but Greek and Latin for twenty-five years and I'm now in charge of every bus in London.

Boris Johnson

184

You can read! It is a great happiness. I totally neglected it while I was in business, which has been the whole of my life, and to such a degree that I cannot now read a page – a warning to all ministers.

Sir Robert Walpole to Henry Fox, when encountering him in the Library at Walpole's country house, Houghton Hall in Norfolk.

The men who do not read are unfit for power.

Michael Foot

When Enoch Powell thought to chide the equally erudite Michael Foot with using the apparent neologism *'remuneration'* in a speech, Foot instantly quoted its appearance in *Love's Labour's Lost.*

(Foot may in fact have been thinking of *Troilus and Cressida* 'O let not virtue seek/Remuneration for the thing it was'. But in any event *'remuneration'* was no neologism; its first recorded appearance was in 1477.)

If you listen to the doctors you are never healthy; if you listen to the theologians you are never saved; and if you listen to the generals you are never safe.

Lord Salisbury

EMOTIONS AND ENORMOUS HATS

There are obvious disadvantages about having women in Parliament. I do not know what is going to be done about their hats. Are they going to wear hats or not...? If you order them not to wear hats you might be absolutely certain that they will insist on wearing them. How is a poor little man to get on with a couple of women wearing enormous hats in front of him?

Rowland Hunt, House of Commons, 1913

Sir William Randal Cremer founded the Inter-Parliamentary Union. He was a pacifist and an early winner of the Nobel Peace Prize. He was not a supporter of votes for women, and he shared Rowland Hunt's hat fixation:

We are told that if women possess the right to vote and assist in the legislation of the House it will infuse into our legislation a humanitarian spirit. This is one of the reasons urged by those who advocate this claim. Some of us, however, have noted the remarkable headgear of women, to adorn which millions of birds have been destroyed and, although it has been pointed out to them that by this practice the most beautiful of the feathered tribe are disappearing, they still continue to wear feathers in their hats. Women have also been told over and over again by some nobler members of their own sex of the horrible suffering undergone by the poor little seals, yet nearly every woman who can afford to do so goes on wearing seal-skin jackets. And these are the people we are asked to admit to the franchise because they will infuse into our legislation a spirit of humanitarianism?

Cremer then shifted up a gear into pure misogyny...

They are privileged all along the line. How many Members have been in an omnibus when it has been raining and the conductor has appealed to them to get out and let a lady in? Men step off the kerb into the gutter to allow a lady to pass clean shod. Whatever view we take of the matter, no one can deny that ladies, because they are ladies, are creatures of privilege.

There are 145 women in the 650-MP membership of the House of Commons, the highest number ever, but still only 22 per cent of the House.

The numbers were generally in single figures from 1918, and in the 20s from 1945 to 1983. They then started to rise: 41 (6.3%) in 1987; 60 (9.2%) in 1992; 120 (18.2%) in 1997; 118 (17.9%) in 2001 and 128 (19.8%) in 2005.

Thirty-three women have been members of the Cabinet, beginning with Margaret Bondfield in 1929–31.

The highest proportion of women in a national parliament is in Rwanda (56%). The rest of the top ten are:

- Andorra, 50%
- Cuba, 45%
- Sweden, 45%
- Seychelles, 44%
- Finland, 43%
- South Africa, 42%
- Netherlands, 40%
- Nicaragua, 40%
- Iceland, 30%

In the international table, the British House of Commons ranks 56th, equal with Malawi. This is behind France (36th with 27%) but ahead of the US (79th on 17%, just ahead of Turkmenistan).

In the House of Lords the proportion is 22%; in the National Assembly for Wales 40%; in the Scottish Parliament 35%; and in the Northern Ireland Assembly 19%. Of UK MEPs, 33% are women.

Sir Hedworth Meux: *It is quite true that women sit on county councils and those sorts of things, but only for two or three hours, and I say that no woman is fit by her physical organisation to stand the strain of Parliament.*

Sir Frederick Banbury: *How about all-night sittings?*

Sir Hedworth Meux: *As the right hon. Baronet says, what about all-night sittings, sitting up until two or three in the morning? 'Who goes home?' It will be a question of 'Who will take me home?'*

House of Commons, 23 October 1918, during debate on the motion *'That, in the opinion of this House, it is desirable that a Bill be passed forthwith making women eligible as Members of Parliament.'*

NANCY ASTOR ON WOMEN

'No one sex can govern alone. I believe that one of the reasons why civilisation has failed so lamentably is that it has had one-sided government.'

'We are not asking for superiority for we have always had that; what we are asking for is equality.'

'Women have got to make the world safe for men since men have made it so darned unsafe for women.'

'I can imagine nothing worse than a man-governed world – except a woman-governed world.'

'In passing, also, I would like to say that the first time Adam had a chance, he laid the blame on a woman.'

'I married beneath me – all women do.'

'*We women talk too much, but even then we don't tell half of what we know.*'

Men as a class will naturally take to politics when they get a chance but women will not because the bent of their minds is different. They live ... by the heart more than the head and the enfranchised servant girl will continue to prefer the novelette to The Times.

Samuel Smith, House of Commons, 1892

The first woman to speak in the House of Lords was Katharine Elliot (Baroness Elliot of Harwood) on 4 November 1958. Her father, Sir Charles Tennant, was born in 1823. Kay Elliot died in 1994 – a span of father and daughter during which there were eight sovereigns and thirty-seven Prime Ministers; which began well before Reform and saw not only women in the House of Lords but the first woman Prime Minister.

FROM *THE MORNING POST*, 21 JANUARY 1913

A great demonstration organised by the National League for Opposing Women's Suffrage was held last night in Queen's Hall. Earl Curzon of Kedleston presided, and the proceedings were of a most enthusiastic character.

Lord Curzon said that '*he held strongly that if any women were to have a vote all should have it, and this would mean that women would govern the country. Such a proposal should not be adopted until it had been put fully and fairly before the electorate, more especially as there was no evidence that the majority of women wanted the vote, while a vast number of them had said that the change would be wholly distasteful to themselves and undesirable for the country.* [Cheers] ... *They must resist it by every means in their power, for they did not want the door to be opened at all, either to a million women walking in dressed up as municipal electors, or to thirteen million women marching as the vanguard of a great army which would, in future, he supposed, take charge of the destinies of the state.'* [Laughter and cheers]

Mr Hobhouse, the Chancellor of the Duchy of Lancaster, said that *'heretofore no State had ever made the bold experiment that England was asked to make, and no condition had ever arisen in which one sex had found itself opposed to the other sex on some vital and unavoidable issue. A second point was that in future decision would not depend on the unanimity of women but also on the present and future disagreement among men. Lord Curzon had pointed out that men were outnumbered to the extent of about a million and a quarter votes, and it was plain that the side which had the majority would have the power to say yea or nay to any proposal which is put forward.* [Cheers]

... It must not be forgotten that there was an enormous majority of women over men. There had always been an exodus of men from this country which had tended to lower

the proportion of men to women, and until that outward stream dried up they would never be able to reverse the position, and if these proposals were carried the predominance of women over men would not only be immutable but impregnable. It was therefore essential that they should defeat this experiment...' [Cheers]

Sir Edward Clarke *'objected to women's suffrage because he believed in an educated democracy.* [Cheers] *The intellectual qualities of men and women were absolutely incomparable. The intellectual equipment of men and women was absolutely different in character. But apart from that he did not want to see our electoral body increased enormously in number by the addition of a class which would lower the tone of the whole electoral body.* [Cheers] *Women were much less educated than men because the natural occupation of the woman in nine-tenths of our classes in society excluded her from the possibility of studying the affairs of the country. If she did she would spoil her home life, she would be a much poorer mother and a less pleasant wife.'* [Cheers]

Mrs Humphrey Ward said: *'As to New Zealand and Finland, what did they matter to us? Let them show another England, with England's vast powers and responsibilities, another State like England governed by women, and they would talk to them.'* [Cheers]

The resolution was then carried with a few dissentients only, amid loud cheering.

The 1919 Plymouth Sutton by-election, forced by the succession to the peerage of the sitting MP, Waldorf Astor, took place on 28 November 1919. It was historic for returning to Westminster Nancy Astor, the first woman to sit in the Commons. (Countess Markievicz was elected for a Dublin constituency in December 1918 but declined to take her seat because of her Irish Republican views.)

Nancy Langhorne, Viscountess Astor, by Zsigismond Kisfaludi Strobl, 1933. The bust was originally commissioned by George Bernard Shaw for his own collection, and presented by Shaw to the Speaker of the House of Commons in 1949

The next day *The Times* pronounced upon the significance of the event, managing to combine guarded approval with lofty condescension...

'Gentlemen of the House of Commons.' This ancient phrase, as old as the Constitution, is now out of date. Its superannuation is but one indication of the tremendous breach in Parliamentary tradition caused by the election to the House of Commons of Viscountess Astor as Member for the Sutton Division of Plymouth. The presence of a woman in the House of Commons as a member was inconceivable no farther back than the years immediately preceding the Great War, so universal was the belief that the one immutable principle of the Constitution was that a member of Parliament should always be a man.

In the many debates on the extension of the franchise to women, one of the most damaging points which its advocates had to encounter was the assertion that it would be followed by a demand for the throwing open of the doors of the House to the opposite sex. All that the advocates could do was to laugh scornfully at the suggestion. Women as members of the House? What next? Was there ever so absurd a thing? Even John Stuart Mill said in his historic pamphlet on 'the Subjugation of Women' – 'the right to share in the choice of those who are to exercise a public trust is altogether a distinct thing from that of competing for the trust itself.'

Will the appearance of a woman in the House of Commons lead to any embarrassments as to seats, procedure and etiquette? Where is Lady Astor to sit? No doubt she will wear her hat in the House, as she would do in a church or chapel. And, if she wears a hat, should she remove it when she rises to speak, as male MPs are bound to do?

There remains the question – how should she be referred to by her fellow members? As Lady Astor is a peeress by marriage, should it be 'the noble lady'? That is a matter of taste. Perhaps Lady Astor would prefer to be spoken of as 'the honourable member for the Sutton Division of Plymouth'.

Nancy Astor took her seat on 1 December 1919, advancing from the Bar of the House to the Table between Lloyd George and Arthur Balfour.

THE LADIES' GALLERY
In the Commons Chamber designed by Barry and destroyed in the air raid on 10 May 1941 there was a hot and stuffy Ladies' Gallery, from where women visitors could observe proceedings – but from behind formidable grilles, which became a powerful symbol of the exclusion of women from Parliament. In 1908 two suffragettes chained themselves to a grille in protest, with cries of '*We have listened behind this insulting grille too long!*'

On that occasion both grille and protestors had to be removed *en bloc* to a committee room to allow the two to be separated. Following a decision of the House in August 1917 the grilles were removed and placed in the Central Lobby, where they can be seen on-screen as part of the backdrop of broadcasters' pieces to camera in the Lobby.

As late as 1912 the plight of women visitors seemed to exercise the government of the day very little:

Mr Sandys: *Asked the hon. Member for St George's-in-the-East, as representing the First Commissioner of Works, whether his attention has been called to the unsatisfactory system of ventilation in the Ladies' Gallery; and whether any improvement can be effected?*

Mr Wedgwood Benn: *No complaint of the ventilation of the Ladies' Gallery has for some time reached the First Commissioner. An independent system for that part of the House was constructed in 1907, upon this it is difficult to effect any improvement.*

Mr Keir Hardie: *Would not an improvement be effected by removing the grille?*

Mr Wedgwood Benn: *I do not think the removal of the grille would affect the ventilation.*

Mr Keir Hardie: *Could the grille be removed?*

Mr Wedgwood Benn: *I do not think that arises out of the question.*

House of Commons, 7 May 1912

Given the history, it was rather surprising that any arrangements at all were made for female visitors. Lord Brougham, in one of the various select committees on the building of the New Palace that tried Sir Charles Barry beyond endurance, said of the possibility that women might observe debates:

If such a proposition is to be made, I enter my protest against it, and shall take the sense of your Lordships upon it, as being contrary to the principle which ought to govern legislative proceedings. I think the ladies would be better employed in almost any other way, than in attending parliamentary debates. I like to see them in their proper places.

Suffragette demonstration in the Ladies' Gallery, House of Commons, on 28 October 1908.
Illustrated London News, 7 November 1908

Women – one half the human race at least – care fifty times more for a marriage than a ministry.
Walter Bagehot, *The English Constitution,* 1867

The Queen is most anxious to enlist every one who can speak or write to join in checking this mad, wicked folly of 'Women's Rights', with all its attendant horrors, on which her poor feeble sex is bent, forgetting every sense of womanly feeling and propriety.

Queen Victoria, in a letter to Theodore Martin, 29 May 1870. Martin was a Scottish poet and biographer; his *Life of His Royal Highness the Prince Consort* won him Victoria's lifelong friendship.

One reason I don't drink is that I want to know when I am having a good time.

Nancy Astor

Take a close up, of a woman past sixty? You might as well take a picture of a relief map of Ireland.

Nancy Astor, to a photographer

And on another occasion: *I refuse to admit I am more than fifty-two, even if that makes my children illegitimate.*

CHANGE AND...?

Change and decay in all around I see...
Henry Francis Lyte, *Abide with Me*, 1847

In England we have come to rely upon a comfortable time-lag of fifty years or a century intervening between the perception that something ought to be done and a serious attempt to do it.
H. G. Wells

CHANGE

When it is not necessary to change, it is necessary not to change.
Lucius Cary, 2nd Viscount Falkland, House of Lords, 1641

Field-Marshal the Duke of Cambridge, 1819–1904,
by Ant in *Vanity Fair*, 1870

All change, for whatever reason, is to be deprecated. There is a time for change, and the time for change is when you can no longer help it.
Field-Marshal the Duke of Cambridge, Commander-in-Chief of the British Army, 1856–95, a strong opponent of overdue Army reform from the 1870s onwards.

Change? Change? Why? Aren't things bad enough as they are?
Lord Salisbury

The main dangers in this life are the people who want to change everything ... or nothing.
Nancy Astor

There is no more striking illustration of the immobility of British institutions than the British House of Commons.
H. H. Asquith, 1926

I see no reason to suppose that these machines will ever force themselves into general use.
The Duke of Wellington, of steam locomotives, 1827

There is only one argument for doing something; the rest are arguments for doing nothing ... it follows that nothing should ever be done for the first time.
F. M. Cornford, the Cambridge philosopher, in 1908

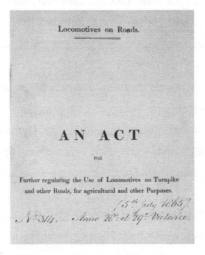

An Act for further regulating the Use of Locomotives on Turnpike and other Roads for agricultural and other purposes: The Locomotive Act 1865, otherwise known as 'the Red Flag Act'

THE RED FLAG ACT...

...was the Locomotive Act 1865. The Locomotive Act 1861 had limited the speed of self-propelled steam road vehicles to 10mph (16km/h), but the 1865 Act reduced this to 4mph (6km/h) in the country and 2mph (3km/h) in towns. Moreover, the 1865 Act also stipulated that each vehicle should have a crew of three: a driver, a stoker and a man with a red flag walking 60 yards ahead of the vehicle (the whistle was not to be sounded nor steam to escape when the vehicle was on the road – to avoid frightening the horses).

In 1865 John Rowbottom became the first victim of the Act, having driven his steam thresher through a village near Doncaster at three in the afternoon. His defence was that he was not travelling but testing some repairs. It was not successful.

The Locomotives on Highways Act 1896 raised the speed to 14mph and removed the requirement for any more crew than the driver. It liberated the infant British motor industry, already lagging well behind the Continent as a result of the 1865 Act.

...AND THE VISIONARIES

Parliament was not wholly supportive of this part of the march of progress. In the same year as the Locomotives on Highways Act, Dr C. K. D. Tanner was saying of motor cars:

In all the places where they have been introduced, they are absolutely found to have become a nuisance.
House of Commons, 1896

They claim the right to drive the public off the roads. Harmless men, women and children, dogs and cattle have all got to fly for their lives at the bidding of one of these slaughtering, stinking engines of iniquity.
Cathcart Wason, House of Commons, 1903.

Wason sat in the New Zealand Parliament from 1876 to 1899. After the failure of his New Zealand business ventures he returned to Scotland and sat for Orkney and Shetland from 1900 to 1921. He was over 6 ft 6 in. tall and passed his time in the Commons by knitting.

Depend upon it, if these motorists and motor cars are not kept in order they will have to leave the roads altogether because in the long run the people will never submit to the intolerable nuisance which has been created.
Charles Cripps KC, House of Commons, 1903

In villages every door and window has to be shut and the occupants cannot even sit in their gardens on account of the dust which is raised by these motor cars. The consequence is that the whole value of their property is destroyed. This also applies in country districts to glass houses used for the cultivation of fruit and flowers... The tremendous dust

raised by them settles on the glass obscuring the sunlight and the fruit and flowers cannot ripen or come into full bloom.
Sir Philip Muntz, House of Commons, 1905

The Lords were on the case too:

The noise of these machines is a public nuisance for they groan, grunt, shiver and stink. The wearing of glasses and leather coats is an affectation and the use of the word 'chauffeur' is intolerable and should be prohibited. The introduction of these needless foreign expressions is odious.
The Earl of Wemyss, House of Lords, 1903

It has had a very bad effect on horse breeding and the displacement of a large number of horses will probably give serious cause for alarm to those who are interested in maintaining the armaments of this country.
Lord Willoughby de Broke, House of Lords, 1908

But clearly there was no need for such alarm:

The spectacle of a regiment of motor cars charging no doubt would be inspiriting but I do not think such a scheme will be likely to prove any permanent advantage to the Army.
Lord Stanley, Financial Secretary to the War Office, 1901

A proposal in 1903 that the speed limit should rise to 20mph was greeted with horror by some:

If this Bill passes as it stands, we shall have to give up the roads entirely to the motoring fraternity.
Ernest Soares, House of Commons, 1903

But there was a counter-argument: if there were to be a speed limit, wouldn't that simply encourage people to go at that speed rather than more slowly?

The imposition of an arbitrary speed limit is a tactical mistake and will not serve the real purpose its advocates have in view.
Lord Balfour of Burleigh, House of Lords, 1903

FORESIGHT

There is not the slightest chance of war with Japan in our lifetime.
Winston Churchill, 1922

It is tempting to bracket this with Field-Marshal Haig's pronouncement in 1926: '*There will always be a place for the well-bred horse on the battlefield.*'

Haig was representative of a substantial body of military opinion. A number of contributions to parliamentary debates in the years after the First World War owed much to the Blackadder principle that: '*When all else fails, a sheer, pig-headed refusal to look facts in the face will always see us through.*'

For example:

Any reduction of cavalry would be a very great mistake indeed. I have served almost all of my life as an infantry-man and I fully realise the tremendous value of cavalry to the infantry ... the numbers of the cavalry instead of being reduced should rather be increased.
Lieutenant-Colonel Acland-Troyte, House of Commons, 1933

If there is one thing which we learned from the War it is the value of cavalry at the beginning of a War ... therefore, it is essential that the numbers should not be further reduced and I hope that ... they will not be mechanised or turned into something else... Our field officers are mounted for the one purpose of being able to go forward and find out exactly the situation. Without cavalry we should be unable to fight a war in Europe or anywhere else.
Lieutenant-Colonel Reginald Applin, House of Commons, 1933

I believe that [the Secretary of State's advisers] *are entirely wrong in thinking they can substitute tanks for cavalry... That seems to be a most extraordinary misreading of the lessons of the War. It seems to me that it would be the most extraordinary misconception of the truth to imagine that in applying science to war the first thing to get rid of is the horse. On the contrary, every advance in science has made the*

horse a more and more indispensable weapon of war. Heavy
artillery fire, heavy machine gun fire, gas, aeroplane obser-
vation – all of these make rapid movement more essential.
Major-General Jack Seely, 1st Lord Mottistone, House of
Commons, 1921

Seely had been in the Cabinet as Secretary of State for War
1912–14. He was the only Cabinet minister to go to the
front in 1914 (and be there four years later). He certainly
knew about cavalry; he commanded the Canadian Cavalry
Brigade in the last major cavalry charge of the First World
War, at the Battle of Moreuil Wood in 1918. He sounds
blinkered on the subject of cavalry, but he was also a
visionary of air power, advocating the formation of the
Royal Flying Corps and even resigning ministerial office
in 1919 over the government's refusal to create an office of
Secretary of State for Air.

Seely had at least the excuse that he was speaking only
three years after the Armistice. But only three years
before the outbreak of the Second World War, with rapid
German rearmament, Commons debates were a good
place to refuse to look facts in the face:

We are quite justified in keeping a nucleus of cavalry which is
the finest arm in the service for training commanding officers.
Brigadier-General Howard Clifton Brown (brother of
Speaker Clifton Brown), House of Commons, 1935

I am perfectly convinced that the role of the cavalry is still as important today as it has been throughout the ages.
Major P. S. Shaw, maiden speech, House of Commons, 1936

It is only too certain that the time may come when we may require the cavalry arm... The total abolition of the cavalry would be a frightful blunder.
Brigadier-General Sir Henry Croft, House of Commons, 1936

My foray into politics ends a slight drought of Draxes here in the Commons. In an earlier deluge, six ancestors graced this place between 1679 and 1880, all representing the long-lost seat of Wareham. One, John Sawbridge Erle-Drax MP, spoke only once during the entire thirty-two years of his Parliamentary career, and that was to ask the Speaker to open the window. Unsurprisingly, he was known as the 'Silent MP'. After his death, he had arranged for The Times *to be delivered daily to his mausoleum through a specially built-in letterbox. Mine is under construction.*
Richard Drax MP, maiden speech, House of Commons, 30 June 2010

I do not object to people looking at their watches when I am speaking. But I strongly object when they start shaking them to make sure they are still going.
Lord Birkett, 1960

You can't have civilisation without sewers, and you can't have Parliament without the Whips.
Speaker Bernard Weatherill, a former government Deputy Chief Whip

Many forms of government have been tried, and will be tried in this world of sin and woe. No one pretends that democracy is perfect or all-wise. Indeed, it has been said that democracy is the worst form of government except all those other forms that have been tried from time to time.
Winston Churchill, House of Commons, 11 November 1947

The only lucid interval he had was the one between his waistcoat and his breeches.
Of Sir Charles Wetherell (1770–1846), Attorney General and notoriously shambolic dresser

CHILD SUPPORT

The first entry in the earliest surviving Journal of the House of Commons, for November 1547, is a bill to make provision for poor men's children.

John Stonehouse (1925–88) was Postmaster General 1968–69 in the Wilson government. In 1976 he was sentenced to seven years for fraud. He was said to have been the only Postmaster General to have sewed his own mailbags.

Sir Codrington Carrington and George Pigott were returned for St Mawes in 1830 with thirteen votes each.

During a debate on the India Bill in 1783 Pepper Arden tried to persuade John Wilkes not to make a speech; if the House was allowed to come to a decision soon it might go in their favour. *'My dear friend,'* said Wilkes, *'I must speak, or I shall otherwise cut a most ridiculous figure tomorrow morning. For two hours ago I sent the speech, which I am about to make, to the Press.'*

> *In politics you should never neglect the possibility that you might have to fall back upon the truth.*
> Michael Foot

> *Might I indicate the difficulty which some of us feel over collective compassion? The good Samaritan had compassion. If two good Samaritans had compassion, that would still be individual compassion, not collective compassion. If the good Samaritan had been obliged by decree of the Roman Emperor to assist the traveller, that would not be compassion at all, because it would be done under obligation.*
> Enoch Powell, House of Commons, 1979

The Official Monster Raving Loony Party, established by Screaming Lord Sutch in 1983, was perhaps the most widely known 'bizarre' party. (One of its law and order policies was to superglue unruly teenagers together.)

But it has had many imitators over the last thirty years, all of which have contested seats at General Elections:

- The Raving Loony Green Giant Party
- The Mongolian Barbecue Great Place to Party Party
- The Rock 'n' Roll Loony Party
- The Dungeons, Death and Taxes Party
- The New Millennium Bean Party
- The I Want To Drop A Blancmange Down Terry Wogan's Y-Fronts Party
- The Miss Great Britain Party
- The Church of the Militant Elvis Party

The best form of government is dictatorship tempered by assassinations.
W. H. Auden

FAREWELL

I say to colleagues whom I am leaving a heartfelt thanks for their comradeship and friendship over the years. I say to those who come after that this is an imperfect institution, as every institution composed of human beings must inevitably be, but it is the bulwark of our liberties. It is the place that ought to matter most of all at the end of the day. When they come here, they should try to recognise that and rise to the occasion. They will be very well served by the staff of the House, and they will come to an institution to which they will feel proud to belong. I say to them that every day they should try to do what I have done and spend at least a minute or two walking through Westminster Hall, the most historic part of this great Palace, where so much of our history has taken place and which should give us all a sense of pride in being British. And so, Mr Deputy Speaker, thank you for the opportunity to make these closing remarks. Ave atque vale.

Sir Patrick Cormack, MP for Cannock, South West Staffordshire and then South Staffordshire 1970–2010, House of Commons, 30 March 2010

Mr Speaker, I depart with mixed feelings. I have heard it said that most MPs stay one Parliament too long, and I thought it better to go while people are still asking 'Why' rather than 'When'. There will be withdrawal symptoms. Leaving now is either the best thing I have ever done or the biggest mistake of my life. At this point, I have no idea which. I do know this, however: I count it a privilege to have been born in a democracy and to have served in this place. The great thing about democracy is that, although harsh things are sometimes said, we are not actually trying to kill each other. Differences are ultimately resolved at the ballot box. One side wins; one side loses; and the loser lives to fight another day. Mr Speaker, those are the last words that I shall speak in this place.

Chris Mullin, MP for Sunderland South 1987–2010, House of Commons, 25 March 2010

Lena Jeger, MP for Holborn and St Pancras South, was canvassing in the 1953 by-election which she won, and reached the top flat of a block in Camden Town. She launched into the great left-wing issue of the day – German rearmament and the threat it posed to international security. She stopped for breath and the woman at the door said:

'*Did you come up in the lift?*'

'*Yes.*'

'*Stinks of pee, doesn't it?*'

'*Yes.*'

'*Can't you stop 'em peeing in the lift?*'

'*Er, no, I don't think I can.*'

'*Well,*' said the prospective voter, '*if you can't stop 'em peeing in our lift, how do you expect me to believe that you can stop the Germans rearming?*'

Democracy means government by discussion, but it is only effective if you can stop people talking.
Clement Attlee

I have never, in this House or elsewhere, so far as I know, said anything discourteous to her, and I do not intend to do so. I do not believe that is the way in which politics should be conducted. That does not mean that we cannot exchange occasional pleasantries. What the right hon. Lady has done today is to lead her troops into battle snugly concealed behind a Scottish Nationalist shield, with the 'boy David' holding her hand. I must say to the right hon. Lady – and I should like to see her smile – that I am even more concerned about the fate of the right hon. Gentleman than I am about her. She can look after herself. But the leader of the Liberal Party – and I say this with the utmost affection – has passed from rising hope to elder statesman without any intervening period whatsoever.

Michael Foot about Margaret Thatcher and David Steel, while winding up the March 1979 confidence debate, which the Callaghan government lost by one vote.

A fortnight with Barbara made 'peace in our time' take on a whole new meaning.

Michael Foot, of arriving with Barbara (later) Castle at Dover on 30 September 1938, the day Chamberlain returned from Munich

Canning's industry was such that he never left a moment unemployed, and such was the clearness of his head that he could address himself almost at the same time to several different subjects with perfect precision and without the least embarrassment. He wrote very fast, but not fast enough for his mind, composing much quicker than he could commit his ideas to paper. He could not bear to dictate, because nobody could write fast enough for him, but on one occasion, when he had the gout in his hand and could not write, he stood by the fire and dictated at the same time a despatch on Greek affairs to George Bentinck and one on South American politics to Howard de Walden, each

214

writing as fast as he could, while he turned from one to the other without hesitation or embarrassment.

Charles Greville's *Diary* for 9 August 1827. Canning was Foreign Secretary 1807–09 and 1822–27, and then Prime Minister. But he died on 8 August 1827, having been Prime Minister for only 119 days.

William Pitt called Canning's speech against a motion in 1798 for peace negotiations with France 'one of the best heard upon any occasion...'

I for my part still conceive it to be the paramount duty of a British member of Parliament to consider what is good for Great Britain... I do not envy that man's feelings, who can behold the sufferings of Switzerland, and who derives from that sight no idea of what is meant by the deliverance of Europe. I do not envy the feelings of that man, who can look without emotion at Italy, plundered, insulted, trampled upon, exhausted, covered with ridicule, and horror, and devastation – who can look at all this, and be at a loss to guess what is meant by the deliverance of Europe? As little do I envy the feelings of that man, who can view the feelings of the peoples of the Netherlands driven into insurrection, and struggling for their freedom against the heavy hand of a merciless tyranny, without entertaining any suspicion of what may be the sense of the word deliverance. Does such a man contemplate Holland groaning under arbitrary oppressions and exactions? Does he turn his eyes to Spain trembling

at the nod of a foreign master? And does the word deliver-
ance still sound unintelligibly in his ear? Has he heard of the
rescue and salvation of Naples, by the appearance and the
triumphs of the British fleet? Does he know that the monar-
chy of Naples retains its existence at the sword's point? And
is his understanding, and his heart, still impenetrable to the
sense and meaning of the deliverance of Europe?

SILENCES

In the middle of the eighteenth century and indeed to a very
much later period, the difficulty was not to check the flow of
oratory but to induce it to flow at all ... awkward silences were
a feature of debate even when the Commons was 'winning the
initiative' against the Crown in the early seventeenth century.
Sir William McKay, *Erskine May's Parliamentary Practice,*
23rd edition

At Nine o' Clock, Mr Speaker removed from his Chair, and
the Committee for the Dispute of new Impositions [sat].
Mr Fuller began first –
A Great Silence.
Journal of the House of Commons, 23 June 1610

The entry for 12 December 1621 begins with the record of:

The House sitting long silent...

On 18 February 1678:

There was a great silence for some time.

Mr Williamson: *Whilst we sit still and say nothing, you must do something in the Chair, or we shall do nothing.*
Mr Powle: *I wonder not at the silence of the Committee, if every man is in the dark as well as I.*
Anchitell Grey MP, *Debates of the House of Commons 1667-94*

'BY THE SLEEPY LAGOON'...

...is the signature tune of *Desert Island Discs*, the national institution in which the programme's guests are invited to choose eight records, a book and a luxury with which to be marooned on a desert island. There have been some interesting book choices:

- Tony Blair: Sir Walter Scott's *Ivanhoe*
- Nick Clegg: *The Leopard*, by Giuseppe di Lampedusa
- Michael Howard: Robert A. Caro's biography of President Lyndon B. Johnson, also chosen by William Hague
- Michael Foot: Byron's *Don Juan*
- Enoch Powell: The Old Testament in Hebrew and the New Testament in Greek
- David Cameron: Hugh Fearnley Whittingstall's *River Cottage Cookbook*

- Nigel Lawson: the works of John Donne, also chosen by Paddy Ashdown
- Shirley Williams: the works of W. H. Auden
- David Davis: the works of the Scottish novelist Iain Banks

A GRACE OF QUEEN ELIZABETH I

God bless our meat,
God guide our ways,
God give us grace,
Our Lord to please
Lord, long preserve in peace and health,
Our gracious Queen Elizabeth.

George Bellin, 1565

ONLINE REFERENCES

The Parliamentary website:
  www.parliament.uk

The Parliamentary Works of Art Collection:
  www.parliament.uk/art

Television coverage and archive:
  www.parliamentlive.tv

The Parliamentary Archives:
  www.parliament.uk/archives

The online Archive catalogue:
  www.portcullis.parliament.uk

Archive learning resources:
  www.parliament.uk/livingheritage